T0353498

Statistics for Bioinformatics

Statistics for Bioinformatics Set

coordinated by
Guy Perrière

Statistics for Bioinformatics

Methods for Multiple Sequence Alignment

Julie Dawn Thompson

First published 2016 in Great Britain and the United States by ISTE Press Ltd and Elsevier Ltd

ISTE Press Ltd
27-37 St George's Road
London SW19 4EU
UK

www.iste.co.uk

Elsevier Ltd
The Boulevard, Langford Lane
Kidlington, Oxford, OX5 1GB
UK

www.elsevier.com

Notices
Knowledge and best practice in this field are constantly changing. As new research and experience broaden our understanding, changes in research methods, professional practices, or medical treatment may become necessary.

Practitioners and researchers must always rely on their own experience and knowledge in evaluating and using any information, methods, compounds, or experiments described herein. In using such information or methods they should be mindful of their own safety and the safety of others, including parties for whom they have a professional responsibility.

To the fullest extent of the law, neither the Publisher nor the authors, contributors, or editors, assume any liability for any injury and/or damage to persons or property as a matter of products liability, negligence or otherwise, or from any use or operation of any methods, products, instructions, or ideas contained in the material herein.

For information on all our publications visit our website at http://store.elsevier.com/

British Library Cataloguing-in-Publication Data
A CIP record for this book is available from the British Library
Library of Congress Cataloging in Publication Data
A catalog record for this book is available from the Library of Congress
ISBN 978-1-78548-216-8

Printed and bound in the UK and US

Contents

Preface

In the past 10 years, biology has been transformed by the development of new genome sequencing technologies known as next-generation sequencing (NGS). This has led to a rapid reduction in the cost of generating genomic data and has made DNA sequencing, RNA-seq and high-throughput screening an increasingly important part of biological and biomedical research. However, the completion of the genome sequences is just a first step toward deciphering the meaning of the genetic "instruction book". The bottleneck is that genome analysis has now shifted to finding efficient and effective ways to analyze the new data in order to leverage their ability to generate insights into the function of biological systems. Whole-genome sequencing is commonly associated with sequencing human genomes, where the genetic data represent a treasure trove for discovering how genes contribute to our health and well-being. However, the scalable, flexible nature of NGS technology makes it equally useful for sequencing any species, such as agriculturally important livestock, plants or disease-related microbes.

The major challenge today is to understand how the genetic information encoded in the genome sequence is translated into the complex processes involved in the organism and the effects of environmental factors on these processes. Bioinformatics plays a crucial role in the systematic interpretation of genome sequence information in association with data from other high-throughput experimental techniques, such as structural genomics, proteomics or transcriptomics. One of the cornerstones of bioinformatics, since its beginnings in the 1980s, has been the comparative analysis of sequences from different organisms known as multiple sequence comparison or multiple sequence alignment (MSA). A variety of computational algorithms have been applied to the sequence alignment problem in diverse domains, most notably in natural language processing. Nevertheless, the alignment of biological sequences involves more than abstract string parsing, since the string of bases or amino acids is a result of complex molecular and evolutionary processes. This book aims to describe the methods that are designed to capture some of this complexity by modeling macromolecular sequences and taking into account their three-dimensional (3D) structures, their cellular functions and their evolution.

The comparison of biological sequences is used to reveal the regions that are conserved in all members of a family of genetic material (genome, gene, RNA, protein, promoter, etc.). This allows identification of regions that have been selected in different organizations during evolution and which are therefore potentially essential for the function at the molecular, cellular or organism levels. As a result, the comparison of nucleic acid or protein sequences has had a major impact on our understanding of the relationships between sequence, structure, function and evolution [LEC 01]. Multiple sequence comparisons or alignments were originally used in evolutionary analyses to explore the phylogenetic relationships between organisms [MOR 06]. Later, new sequence database search methods exploited multiple alignments to detect more and more distant homologues [ALT 97]. MSAs of nucleic acid or protein sequences are also used to highlight conserved functional features and to identify major evolutionary events, such as duplications, recombinations or mutations. They have led to a significant improvement in predictions of both 3D fold [MOU 05] and function [WAT 05]. Of course, in the current era of complete genome sequences, it is now possible to perform comparative multiple sequence analysis at the genome level [DEW 06].

Such studies have important implications in numerous fields in biology. Nucleic acid divergence is used as a molecular clock to study organism divergence under the evolutionary forces of natural selection, genetic drift, mutation and migration [FEL 04], with applications from the scientific classification or taxonomy of species to genetic fingerprinting. Conserved sequence features or markers are used to characterize groups of individuals in population genetics [SCH 15]. Genotype/phenotype correlations can reveal candidate genes associated with a particular trait (e.g. plant height) or inherited disease, such as schizophrenia or asthma [MOR 12]. In drug discovery, a protein family perspective can identify specific structural or functional features that facilitate protein–ligand interaction studies for high-throughput virtual compound screening methods [LEN 00]. Thus, multiple alignments now play a fundamental role in most of the computational methods used in genomic or proteomic projects for gene identification and the functional characterization of the gene products.

The first part of this book will introduce the fundamental concepts required to understand the development of MSA methods, including a description of the main characteristics of biological sequences and a more complete definition of what a "multiple sequence alignment" is and why it is so important. The second part of the book will then describe the traditional methods that are most widely used for the construction and analysis of MSAs. The literature is vast, and hence our presentation of these topics is necessarily selective. We will address the problems of alignment construction and survey the range of practical techniques for computing MSAs, with a focus on practical methods that have demonstrated good performance on real-world benchmarks. The third part of the book will then introduce the new bioinformatics approaches that are being developed in order to manage and extract pertinent information from the mass of data generated by the new high-throughput genome sequencing technologies.

Julie DAWN THOMPSON
September 2016

PART 1

Fundamental Concepts

Introduction

1.1. Biological sequences: DNA/RNA/proteins

Some basic concepts in biology are necessary for understanding almost any part of this book, so this chapter represents a brief primer on the key ideas and concepts. For many readers, this will be familiar territory and in this case, they may want to skip this section and go directly to section 1.2.

A genome is the genetic material of an organism. Each genome contains the entire set of hereditary instructions needed to build that organism and allow it to grow and develop. The instructions in the genome are encoded in very long DNA molecules, organized into pairs of chromosomes. The chromosomes are made up of chains of four nucleotide bases, adenine (A), guanine (G), thymine (T) and cytosine (C). The human genome, for example, contains 23 pairs of chromosomes and has more than 3 billion base pairs. The chromosomes can be further broken down into smaller pieces of code called genes, including over 20,000 protein-coding genes and many thousands of non-coding RNA (ncRNA) genes.

RNA is another molecule consisting of chains of four nucleotide bases, in this case adenine (A), cytosine (C), guanine (G) or uracil (U). RNA plays a key role in all steps of gene expression as an intermediate carrier of genetic information and as a functional intermediate of the expression cascade that amplifies single genes into many copies of the encoded proteins. Many ncRNAs (transfer RNA (tRNA), snRNA, miRNA, etc.) are also involved in direct regulation of transcription and translation. The function of an RNA molecule depends mostly on its tertiary structure and this structure is generally more conserved than the primary sequence [WOE 93].

Proteins are made up of chains of amino acid residues and can vary in length from about 20 to over 10,000. There are 20 different amino acids, usually represented by a single letter code. Proteins perform a wide variety of biological functions in organisms, from catalysis of biochemical reactions, transport of nutrients or recognition and transmission of signals to structural and mechanical roles within the cell. As a result, one of the earliest and most important applications of bioinformatics was the study of the relationships between the sequence of a protein and its 3D structure, biological function and evolution. A direct relationship between sequence similarity and conservation of 3D structure has been clearly established [KOE 02]. However, the relation between fold and function is much more complex [WAT 05], since gene function can be described at many levels, ranging from biochemical function, via macromolecular complexes to cellular processes and pathways, up to the organ or organism level.

1.2. From DNA to RNA and proteins

The Central Dogma of Molecular Biology [CRI 58] states that the genetic information encoded in DNA is transcribed to generate RNA and that these RNAs are then translated to form proteins that perform cellular functions. The RNA intermediary between DNA and protein is a messenger type of RNA, or mRNA. The Central Dogma stipulates that no genetic information is transferred from protein to protein, protein to RNA or protein to DNA. Over the last 50 years, many discoveries have challenged the Central Dogma and the fixed, deterministic view of DNA. They have revealed that, while the essential elements of the Central Dogma still hold, it is a rather oversimplistic model. Some examples of alternative information pathways have been observed. For example, reverse transcription from RNA into DNA is performed by retroviruses [DE 05] or retrotransposons [MOU 05]. Also, some virus species have their entire genome encoded in the form of RNA [AHL 06]; thus, their information flow consists only of RNA to protein. Many ncRNAs in an organism achieve a functional state capable of affecting the phenotype of the organism without ever being translated into a protein [SZA 15]. Thus, their information flow consists only of DNA to RNA. As a final example, prions are proteins that propagate themselves by making conformational changes in other molecules of the same type [TUI 10], affecting the behavior of the protein. In fungi, this change can be passed from one generation to the next, i.e. protein to protein.

Thus, the Central Dogma of Molecular Biology inspired by classical work in prokaryotic organisms accounts for only part of the genetic agenda of complex eukaryotes. In fact, gene expression is subject to a regulatory network of a complexity that is only just being realized. But, translation of the DNA genes to RNA or protein sequences is only the first step in the synthesis of functionally active molecules and further processing is required to obtain the final 3D structure and biochemical function of the gene product.

1.3. RNA sequence, structure and function

RNAs are single stranded polynucleotide molecules that often fold on themselves by base pairing to form structures called hairpin loops. Thus, most RNA molecules adopt specific tertiary structures. An example is shown in Figure 1.1.

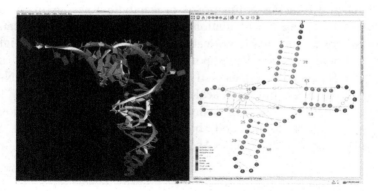

Figure 1.1. *Different levels of RNA structure. For a color version of the figure, see www.iste.co.uk/thompson/statistics.zip*

COMMENT ON FIGURE 1.1.– *A screenshot showing the crystal structure of yeast phenylalanine tRNA in the Assemble2 software www.bioinformatics.org/assemble. tRNAs are polynucleotides of about 60–95 nucleotides, which exhibit a cloverleaf-like structure consisting of a stem and three main loops. The tertiary L-shaped structure interacts with ribosomes, aminoacyl tRNA synthetases, etc.*

Structural studies and comparative sequence analyses have suggested that biological RNAs are largely modular in nature, composed primarily of conserved structural building blocks or motifs [LEO 03] of secondary (helices, and internal, external or junction loops) and tertiary (coaxial stacks, kissing hairpin loops, ribose zippers, etc.) structures. The secondary structure elements are significantly more stable and form faster than the tertiary interactions. Tertiary structure in RNA occurs via interactions involving two helices, two unpaired regions, or one unpaired region and a double-stranded helix. At the same time, detailed analysis of water, metal, ligand and protein binding to RNA has revealed the effect of these moieties on folding and structure formation [HOL 05]. It is this 3D structure that largely determines the functional activity of the RNA.

RNA plays numerous key roles in biological processes, including protein synthesis, mRNA splicing, transcriptional regulation and retroviral replication. mRNA is a single-stranded molecule used as the template for protein translation. Other ncRNAs have been discovered more recently that have functional or catalytic roles in many cell processes including the regulation of transcription, DNA replication and RNA processing and modification [SZA 15]. These include highly abundant and functionally important RNAs such as tRNAs and ribosomal RNAs (rRNAs), as well as snoRNAs, microRNAs, siRNAs, snRNAs, exRNAs, piRNAs, scaRNAs and the long ncRNAs. The number of ncRNAs encoded within the human genome is unknown; however, transcriptomic and bioinformatic studies suggest the existence of thousands of ncRNAs [ENC 07].

1.4. Protein sequence, structure and function

Classified by biological function, proteins include the enzymes, which are responsible for catalyzing the thousands of chemical reactions of the living cell; structural proteins such as tubulin, keratin or collagen; transport proteins such as hemoglobin; regulatory proteins such as transcription factors or cyclins that regulate the cell cycle; signaling molecules such as some hormones and their receptors; defensive proteins such as antibodies that are part of the immune system; and proteins that perform mechanical work, such as actin and myosin, the contractile muscle proteins.

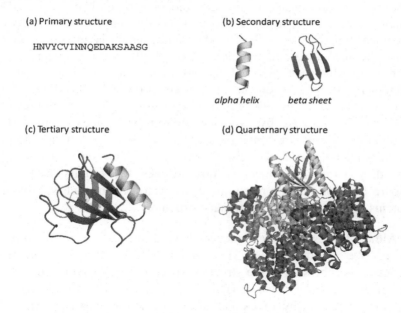

Figure 1.2. *Different levels of protein structure. For a color version of the figure, see www.iste.co.uk/thompson/statistics.zip*

COMMENT ON FIGURE 1.2.– *The ribbons represent examples of the four levels of protein structure. (a) The linear sequence of amino acid residues defines the primary structure. (b) Secondary structure consists of regions of regularly repeating conformations of the peptide chain, such as alpha helices and beta sheets. (c) Tertiary structure describes the shape of the fully folded polypeptide chain. The example shown (PDB: 1btn) was visualized with the Pymol viewer. (d) Quaternary structure refers to the arrangement of two or more polypeptide chains into a multisubunit molecule (PDB: 4hat).*

Every protein molecule has a characteristic 3D shape or conformation, known as its native state. Fibrous proteins, such as collagen and keratin, consist of polypeptide chains arranged in roughly parallel fashion along a single linear axis, thus forming tough, usually water-insoluble, fibers or sheets. Globular proteins, e.g. many of the known enzymes, show a tightly folded structural geometry approximating the shape of an ellipsoid or sphere. The precise 3D structure of a protein molecule is generally required for proper biological function, since the specific conformation is needed for cell factors to recognize and interact with it. If the tertiary structure is altered, e.g. by such physical factors as extremes of temperature, changes in pH or variations in salt concentration, the molecule is said to be denatured; it usually exhibits reduction or loss of biological activity. The process by which a protein sequence assumes its functional shape or conformation is known as folding. Protein folding can be considered as a hierarchical process, in which sequence defines secondary structure, which in turn defines the tertiary structure (Figure 1.2). Individual protein molecules can then interact with other proteins to form complex quaternary structures.

Although most protein sequences have a unique 3D confirmation, the inverse is not true. A 3D structure does not have a unique sequence, i.e. the size of the structure space is much smaller than the size of the sequence space. It is commonly assumed that it is thought that the vast majority of extant proteins will fall into only around 1,000 common folds (where a fold is a general consensus of the tertiary structure) [KOO 02]. A direct relationship has been clearly established between protein sequence similarity and conservation of 3D structure [KOE 02]. Although exceptions exist, it is generally believed that when two proteins share 50% or higher sequence identity, they will generally share the same structural fold. However, in the so-called "twilight zone" of 20–30% sequence identity, it is no longer possible to reliably infer structural similarity [KHO 15].

The relation between 3D fold and function is much more complex and the same fold is often seen to have different functions [MIL 15]. After translation, the posttranslational modification of amino acids can extend the range of functions of the protein by attaching to it other biochemical functional groups such as acetate, phosphate, various lipids and carbohydrates by changing the chemical nature of an amino acid or by making structural changes, such as the formation of disulfide bridges [XU 16]. With respect to enzymes, local active-site mutations, variations in surface loops and recruitment of additional domains accommodate the diverse substrate specificities and catalytic activities observed within several superfamilies. Conversely, different folds can perform the same function, sometimes with the same catalytic cluster and mechanism (for example trypsin and subtilisin proteinases). These results highlight the need to look beyond simple evolutionary relationships, at the details of a molecule's active sites, to assign specific functions.

1.5. Sequence evolution

During evolution, random mutagenesis events take place, which change the gene sequences that encode RNA and proteins. There are several different types of mutation that can occur. Point mutations substitute a single nucleic or amino acid residue for another one. Residue insertions and deletions also occur, involving a single residue up to several hundred residues. Other evolutionary mechanisms at work in nature include genetic recombination, where DNA strands are broken and rejoined to form new combinations of genes. Some of these evolutionary changes will make a gene non-functional, e.g. most mutations of active site residues in an enzyme, or mutations that prevent the molecule from folding correctly. If this happens to a gene that carries out an essential process, the cell (or organism) containing the mutation will die. As a result, residues that are essential for a gene's function, or that are needed for the molecule to fold correctly, are conserved over time. Occasionally, mutations occur that give rise to new functions. This is one of the ways that new traits and eventually species may come about during evolution.

By comparing related sequences and looking for those residues that remain the same in all of the members in the family, we can predict which residues might be essential for function. Thus, multiple sequence comparison or alignment has become a fundamental tool in many different domains in modern molecular biology, from evolutionary studies to prediction of 2D/3D structure, molecular function and intermolecular interactions, etc. By placing the sequence in the framework of the overall family, multiple alignments not only identify important structural or functional motifs that have been conserved through evolution but can also highlight particular non-conserved features resulting from specific events or perturbations [LEC 01].

1.6. MSA: basic concepts

In the most general terms, an alignment represents a set of sequences using a single-letter code for each amino acid (for protein sequences) or nucleotide (for DNA/RNA sequences) residue (Figure 1.3). Each horizontal row in the alignment represents a single sequence and structurally, functionally or evolutionarily equivalent residues are aligned vertically. When the sequences are of different lengths, insertion–deletion events are postulated to explain the variation and gap characters are introduced into the alignment.

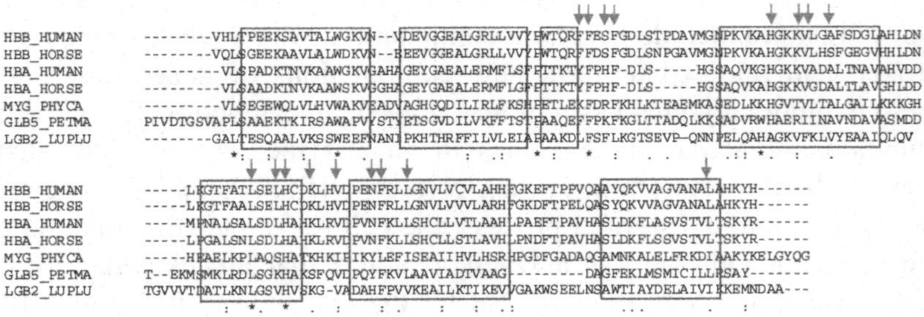

Figure 1.3. *Example alignment of a set of seven hemoglobin domain sequences. For a color version of the figure, see www.iste.co.uk/thompson/statistics.zip*

COMMENT ON FIGURE 1.3.– *The alignment shows the seven helical structures (red boxes) and the conserved residues forming the heme pocket of the beta subunit (blue arrows). The symbols below the alignment indicate conserved positions: * = fully conserved identical residue; : = fully conserved "similar" residue; . = partially conserved "similar" residue.*

1.6.1. *Pairwise versus multiple alignment*

There exist two main categories of sequence alignment: pairwise (or the alignment of two sequences) and multiple alignments. Pairwise alignments are most commonly used in database search programs such as BLAST [ALT 97] and FASTA [PEA 90] in order to detect homologs of a novel sequence. Multiple alignments, containing from three to several hundred sequences, are more computationally complex than pairwise alignments and, in general, simultaneous alignment of more than a few sequences is rarely attempted. Instead, a series of pairwise alignments are performed and amalgamated into a multiple alignment. Nevertheless, multiple alignments have the advantage of providing an overall view of the family, thus helping to decipher the evolutionary history of the protein family. MSAs are useful in identifying conserved patterns in protein families, which may not be evident from pairwise alignments. They are also used in the determination of domain organization, to help predict protein secondary/tertiary structure, and in phylogenetic studies. MSA applications will be discussed in more detail in Chapter 2.

1.6.2. *Local versus global alignment*

Sequence alignments can be further divided into global alignments that align the complete sequences and local alignments that identify only the most similar segments or sequence patterns (motifs). While global alignment algorithms produce more accurate alignments for proteins of similar length, local alignment algorithms are better at identifying similar regions within sequences when the sequences are not related over their entire length.

Alignments are produced by a wide variety of programs, known as "aligners", sometimes as a side product of the main function of the program. In local alignments, produced by aligners such as Dialign [MOR 98], the conserved motifs are identified and the rest of the sequences are included for information only. Thus, only a subset of the residues is actually aligned. In global alignments, typically produced by aligners such as ClustalW [THO 94], all the residues in both sequences participate in the alignment. By placing the sequence in the context of the overall family, the global alignment permits not only a horizontal analysis of the sequence over its entire length, but also a vertical view of the evolution of the protein. The global alignment thus represents a powerful integrative tool that addresses a variety of biological problems, ranging from key functional residue detection to the evolution of a protein family.

1.7. Multiple sequence alignment applications

Multiple alignments play a fundamental role in most areas of modern molecular biology, from shaping our basic conceptions of life and its evolutionary processes to providing the foundation for the new biotechnology industry. In this chapter, we will discuss some of the most important applications, including phylogeny, RNA/protein structure prediction, functional characterization and, more recently, complete genome assembly and annotation, comparative genomics, etc.

1.7.1. *Phylogenetic studies*

One of the earliest applications of multiple sequence alignments was phylogenetics, or the science of estimating the evolutionary past. In the case of molecular phylogeny, this is done based on the comparison of DNA, RNA or protein sequences. For example, the accepted universal tree of life, in which the living world is divided into three domains (bacteria, archaea and eucarya), was constructed from comparative analyses of rRNA sequences [WOE 00].

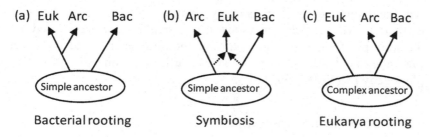

Figure 1.4. *Alternative hypotheses for the rooting of the tree of life*

According to this rRNA-based tree, billions of years ago a universal common ancestor gave rise to the two microbial branches, the archaea and bacteria and later, the archaea gave rise to the eukarya (Figure 1.4(a)). This universal tree is still widely used, although some of the main features have been challenged by subsequent analyses [FOR 15]. For example, comparisons of whole-genome sequences suggested that the eukaryotic lineage arose from metabolic symbiosis between eubacteria and methanogenic archaea (Figure 1.4(b)). In this case, early eukaryotes would be a chimera of eubacterial and archaeal genes, in which the operational genes were primarily from the eubacteria, and the informational genes from the archaea. But some important eukaryotic genes have no obvious predecessors in either the archaeal or the bacterial lines, and an alternative has been suggested where prokaryotes would have evolved by simplification of a more complex ancestral genome (Figure 1.4(c)). In a comprehensive study of ribosomal genes in complete genomes from 66 different species, the archaeal ribosome appeared to be a small-scale model of the eukaryotic genes in terms of protein composition [LEC 02], which would support the eukaryotic-rooting tree.

The methods for calculating phylogenetic trees fall into two general categories [PAG 98]. These are distance-matrix methods, also known as clustering or algorithmic methods (e.g. UPGMA or neighbor joining), and discrete data methods, also known as tree searching methods (e.g. parsimony, maximum likelihood, Bayesian methods). All of these methods use distance measures based on the multiple sequence alignment and the strategy used to construct the alignment can have a large influence on the resulting phylogeny [MOR 97].

1.7.2. *Comparative genomics*

With the widespread availability of complete genome sequences, it is now possible to perform comparative multiple sequence analysis at the genome level [DEW 12]. As genomes evolve, large-scale evolutionary processes, such as recombination, deletion or horizontal transfer, cause frequent genome rearrangements [SHA 05]. Comparative analyses of complete genomes present a comprehensive view of the level of conservation of gene order, or synteny, between different genomes, and thus provide a measure of organism relatedness at the genome scale [DAR 04]. Examples of such analyses include a study showing that about 60% of genes are conserved between fruit flies and humans [RUB 00], or a comparison of human disease mutations in a large set of 100 vertebrate genomes [JOR 15].

A number of software tools have been developed to explore the similarities and differences between genomes at different levels. Because of the volume and nature of the data involved, almost all the visualization tools in this field use a web interface to access large databases of precomputed sequence comparisons and annotations, e.g. GenomeVista [POL 14], Ensembl [KER 15], UCSC [SPE 15]. For example, Figure 1.5 shows an 12 Mb region of the human chromosome 12, together with homologous regions of other vertebrate genomes, displayed using the UCSC genome browser.

This particular region was identified by genome-wide single-nucleotide polymorphism (SNP) based mapping in families with mutations involved in Bardet–Biedl syndrome (BBS), a genetically heterogeneous ciliopathy [STO 06].

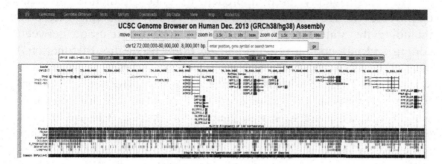

Figure 1.5. *UCSC genome browser display*

COMMENT ON FIGURE 1.5.– *The display shows a 12 Mb region of homozygosity that segregated with the disease phenotype in different sibships in families with BBS mutations. The region contains 23 known genes, including the BBS10 gene, a major locus for BBS. Syntenic regions from chimp, dog, mouse and other organisms are shown at the bottom of the display.*

1.7.3. Gene prediction and validation

One important aspect in biotechnology is gene discovery and target validation for drug discovery. At the time of writing, over 74,000 genomes are either complete or being determined, including more than 55,000 bacteria, 1,000 archaea and 12,000 eukarya (gold.jgi.doe.gov). Unfortunately, biological interpretation is not keeping pace with this avalanche of raw sequence data and there is still a real need for accurate and fast tools to analyze these sequences and, especially, to find genes and determine their functions. Unfortunately, finding genes in a genomic sequence is far from being a trivial problem. It has been estimated that at least 50% of the protein sequences predicted from eukaryotic genomes contain suspicious regions due to errors in the prediction of the exon/intron structures [GUI 06].

The most widely used approach to gene prediction involves employing heterogeneous information from different methods, including the statistical analysis of a bias in codon usage between coding and non-coding regions and *ab initio* prediction of functional sites in the DNA sequence, such as splice sites, promoters or start and stop codons [ZIC 15]. Most current methods of detection of a signal that may represent the presence of a functional site use position-weight matrices, consensus sequences or hidden Markov models (HMM). The reliability and accuracy of these methods depends critically on the quality of the underlying multiple alignments. For prokaryotic genomes, these combined methods are highly successful, identifying over 95% of the genes [AGG 02], although the exact determination of the start site location remains more problematic because of the absence of relatively strong sequence patterns. The process of predicting genes in higher eukaryotic genomes is complicated by several factors, including complex gene organization, the presence of large numbers of introns and repetitive elements and the sheer size of the genomic sequence. It has been shown that comparison of the *ab initio* predicted exons with protein, EST or cDNA databases can improve the sensitivity and specificity of the overall prediction. For example, in the reannotation of the *Mycoplasma pneumoniae* genome [DAN 00], sequence alignments were used in the prediction of N/C-terminal extensions to the original protein reading frame. Sequence alignments have also been combined with experimental proteomics data in an orthoproteogenomics approach in order to refine gene annotations in multiple genomes simultaneously [GAL 09].

Multiple alignments have also been exploited in methods for automatic protein quality control, for example in the SIBIS program [KHE 14].

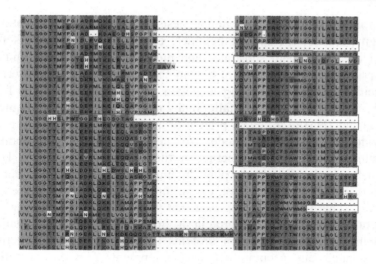

Figure 1.6. *Detection of sequence errors in a set of hypothetical proteins from the Uniprot database using SIBIS . For a color version of the figure, see www.iste.co.uk/thompson/statistics.zip*

COMMENT ON FIGURE 1.6.– *Multiple alignment showing reliable sequence segments and potential errors highlighted by red boxes.*

SIBIS detects sequence inconsistencies due to natural variants or sequence prediction errors based on the evolutionary information in multiple sequence alignments. It is based on a Bayesian framework, combined with Dirichlet mixture models, and can be used to estimate the probability of observing specific amino acids and to detect inconsistent or wrong sequence segments. Figure 1.6 shows an example involving a large set of sequences from the UniProt database, corresponding to hypothetical proteins. Integration of quality control methods like SIBIS in automatic analysis pipelines is crucial for the robust inference of structural, functional and phylogenetic information from these sequences.

1.7.4. Protein structure and function

Knowing the molecular determinants of protein structure and function has many critical applications in biology and medicine, for example, to guide efficient mutagenesis, interpret patient mutations, design potential therapeutic peptides, extract functional motifs that predict functions and substrates and measure the molecular, clinical and population-wide action of human coding variations. Because it is difficult and time consuming to obtain experimental structures from methods such as X-ray crystallography and protein Nuclear Magnetic Resonance (NMR) for every protein of interest, *in silico* modeling can provide useful structural models for generating hypotheses about a protein's function and directing further experimental work. Here again, multiple alignments play an important role in a number of aspects of the characterization of the three-dimensional structure of a protein. The most accurate *in silico* method for determining the structure of an unknown protein is homology structure modeling. Sequence similarity between proteins usually indicates a structural resemblance, and accurate sequence alignments provide a practical approach for structure modeling, when a 3D structural prototype is available. For models based on distant evolutionary relationships, it has been shown that multiple sequence alignments often improve the accuracy of the structural prediction [MOU 05]. Multiple sequence alignments are also used to significantly increase the accuracy of *ab initio* prediction methods for both 2D [DRO 15] and 3D [ALL 01] structures by taking into account the overall consistency of putative features. Similarly, multiple alignments are also used to improve the reliability of other predictions, such as transmembrane helices [RAT 13]. More detailed structural analyses also exploit the information in multiple alignments. For example, functionally important regions, such as binding surfaces common to protein families, can be defined on the basis of sequence conservation patterns and knowledge of the shared fold [LUA 15].

To further characterize the functions of a novel protein, another widely used strategy in most genome annotation projects is to search the sequence databases for related proteins and to propagate the structural/functional annotation from one to the other. In this case, evolutionary relationships between proteins can take into account the full-length sequences, e.g. in the ConFunc system [WAS 08], or can look for similarities to known domains in precompiled databases, such as Interpro [MIT 15]. These databases contain representations such as profiles or HMMs of individual protein domains based on multiple alignments of known sequences. For a more complete review of homology-based annotation methods, see [LOE 09].

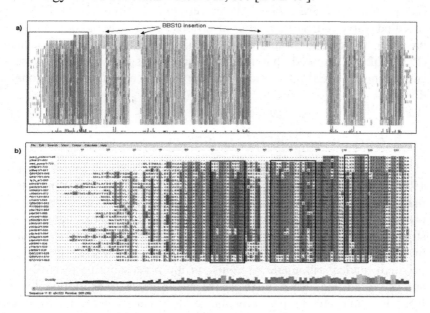

Figure 1.7. *Multiple alignment of the BBS10 protein and homologs found in in-depth database searches. For a color version of the figure, see www.iste.co.uk/thompson/statistics.zip*

COMMENTS ON FIGURE 1.7.– *a) Overview of complete protein, showing global organization, including three insertions specific to BBS10 and the N-terminal deletion due to an error in the exon prediction of the gene. The red box indicates the region shown in (b). Residues are colored according to the coloring scheme used in ClustalX [THO 97]. (b) N-terminal region of the BBS10 alignment. The black boxes indicate the positions of ATP binding site motifs, as defined in the ProSite database.*

Genome annotation systems such as GeneQuiz [HOE 00], BASys [VAN 05] or MicroScope [VAL 14] use multiple alignments to reliably incorporate information from more distant homologues and provide a more detailed description of protein function. As an illustration, Figure 1.7 shows a multiple alignment of the BBS10 protein and related sequences. The BBS10 sequence shows some similarity (approximately 11% residue identity) to several chaperonin-like proteins that are found only in vertebrates, although the MACS revealed three BBS10-specific insertions. A 3D homology model based on the crystal structure of the chaperonin from Thermococcus (PDB:1q2vA) showed that the three insertions are spatially close, suggesting potential interactions and the existence of a new functional domain.

1.7.5. *RNA structure and function*

Since the elucidation of DNA structure by Watson and Crick in 1953, DNA and proteins were generally deemed the dominant macromolecules in the living cell, with RNA only aiding in creating proteins from the DNA blueprint. More recently, a large number of studies have demonstrated multiple roles for RNA beyond a simple message or transfer molecule [CEC 14]. These include the importance of small nuclear ribonucleoproteins in the processing of pre-mRNA and RNA editing, RNA interference and reverse transcription from RNA in eukaryotes in the maintenance of telomeres in the telomerase reaction. RNA secondary and tertiary structure studies are thus crucial to the understanding of complex biological systems. Structure and structural transitions are important in many areas, such as posttranscriptional regulation of gene expression, intermolecular interaction and dimerization, splice site recognition and ribosomal frame shifting. The function of an RNA molecule depends mostly on its tertiary structure and this structure is generally more conserved than the primary sequence. The determination of RNA 3D structure is a limiting step in the study of RNA structure–function relationships because it is very difficult to crystallize and/or obtain nuclear magnetic resonance spectrum data for large RNA molecules. Currently, a reliable prediction of RNA secondary and tertiary structure from its primary sequence is mainly derived from multiple alignments, searching among members of a family for compensatory base changes that would maintain base pairedness in equivalent regions. For example, the Assemble tool [JOS 10] proposes a graphical interface to analyze, manipulate and build complex 3D RNA architectures (Figure 1.8).

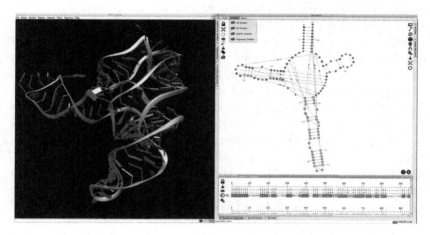

Figure 1.8. *Assemble (www.bioinformatics.org/assemble) display of a multiple alignment of an S-box (SAM-I) riboswitch from Bacillus subtilis. For a color version of the figure, see www.iste.co.uk/thompson/statistics.zip*

COMMENTS ON FIGURE 1.8.– *Multiple sequence alignment, secondary and tertiary structure (PDB:4KQY). Inside the multiple alignment, the bracket notation is such that the regular parentheses ("and") denote the helical Watson–Crick pairs and the "<" and ">" characters specify non-Watson–Crick base pairs typical of RNA motifs.*

These methods have been demonstrated by successful predictions of RNA structures for tRNAs, 5S and 16S rRNAs, RNase P RNAs, small nuclear RNAs (snRNAs) and other RNAs, such as group I and group II introns.

The phylogenetic comparative methods are often supported by complementary, theoretical structure calculations. The goal here is to predict 3D RNA structures directly from the sequence. These *de novo* modeling methods include all atom based methods that predict structure by simulating the folding process using force fields and molecular mechanics. Various software packages such as CHARMM [BRO 09] have force fields optimized to run RNA simulations.

However, these simulations are computationally expensive and therefore limited to small RNAs. This problem can be alleviated by using coarse-grained methods that reduce the computational time by simplifying how the nucleotides are represented in the model, for example Vfold [XU 14] among others. In addition, there are methods that represent RNA as graphs, which further reduce the sampling space by representing each helix as a stick or a cylinder [KIM 14]. The accuracy of coarse-grained methods depends on the choice of representation and the scoring function. Fragment-assembly methods build RNA models by assembling short fragments extracted from structural databases. MC-Sym [PAR 08] assembles structures using a library of nucleotide cyclic motifs and Monte Carlo sampling. RNAComposer [POP 12] can build large RNAs using a fragment database (RNA FRABASE). Both MC-Sym and RNAComposer are fully automated and available as Web servers.

1.7.6. *Interaction networks*

In the systems biology view of cellular function, each biological entity is seen in the context of a complex network of interactions. Powerful experimental techniques, such as the yeast two-hybrid system or tandem-affinity purification coupled with mass spectrometry, are used to determine protein–protein interactions systematically. In parallel with these developments, a number of computational techniques have been designed for predicting protein interactions. The performance of the Rosetta method, which relies on the observation that some interacting proteins have homologues in another organism fused into a single protein chain, was improved using multiple sequence alignment information and global measures of hydrophobic core formation [BON 01]. A measure of the similarity between phylogenetic trees of protein families was also used to predict pairs of interacting proteins [OCH 15].

Homologous template-based predictors have also been developed that use known complexes where one of the interacting partners is homologous to the query protein. The interface via which the homologous protein interacts is assumed to be an indicator of where the corresponding interface might be found on the query protein.

Coevolution strategies have also been used to detect interfaces. The coevolution principle suggests that mutations on one protein in a complex are often compensated for by correlated mutations within the same chain or on a binding partner. Such correlated mutations are assumed to maintain the stability of the protein or protein–protein complex. By creating MSAs of the input proteins, we identify the columns that appear to change in concert indicating spatial proximity. Since protein interaction data and sequence information is increasing exponentially, it is likely that this will further improve the quality and the applicability of coevolution predictors in the future [ESM 15].

Such large-scale identification of Protein-Protein Interactions (PPIs), either experimentally or computationally, generates hundreds of thousands of interactions, many of which are collected together in specialized biological databases, such as the Database of Interacting Proteins, Biomolecular Interaction Network Database, IntAct Molecular Interaction Database, Molecular Interactions Database or IntAct. Meta-databases and prediction databases include many PPIs that are predicted using several techniques, for example STRING.

1.7.7. Genetics

A considerable effort is now underway to relate human phenotypes to variation at the DNA level. Human genetic variation is represented by SNPs, small insertions/deletions or larger-scale chromosome rearrangements. Many of them are believed to cause phenotypic differences between individuals [FRE 14]. Today's NGS technologies afford the opportunity to sequence all nucleotides in the human exome and even in the human genome. Given that more than three-quarters of the known disease-causing variants are located in the exome, and considering the cost and technical challenges in analyzing the whole genome sequence data, the focus of present research is primarily on whole exome sequencing (WES). While WES at the medical sequencing level is still expensive, it is becoming more affordable. Cost will not likely be a major barrier in the near future, and the data analysis is becoming less tedious. The most difficult challenge at the heart of medical sequencing is interpreting the findings. Each exome contains about 13,500 single nucleotide variants that affect the amino acid sequence, and a large number are expected to be functional variants. The daunting task is to distinguish the variants that are pathogenic from those that have minimal or no discernible clinical effects.

One of the main goals of medical genetics research is therefore to understand the genetics of human phenotype variation and especially the genetic basis of complex diseases, thus providing a basis for assessing susceptibility to diseases and designing individual therapy. Although a large number of variations may be functionally neutral, others may have deleterious effects on the regulation or the functional activity of specific gene products. Non-synonymous SNPs (nsSNPs) that lead to an amino acid change in the protein product are of particular interest because they account for nearly half of the known genetic variations related to human inherited disease [STE 03]. With more and more data available, it has become imperative to predict the phenotype of a variant *in silico*. Computational tools are therefore being developed, which use structural information or evolutionary information from multiple sequence alignments to predict a phenotypic effect and to identify disease-associated variants, e.g. KD4v for nsSNPs [LUU 12] or KD4i for insertions and deletions [BER 14].

1.7.8. *Drug discovery and design*

The structural and functional analyses described above provide an opportunity to identify the proteins associated with a particular disease, which are therefore potential drug targets. Rational drug design strategies can then be directed to accelerate and optimize the drug discovery process using experimental and virtual (computer-aided drug discovery) methods. Recent advances in the computational analyses of enzyme structures and functions have improved the strategies used to modify enzyme specificities and mechanisms by site-directed mutagenesis and to engineer biocatalysts through molecular reassembly.

For example, vitamin D analogs have been proposed for the treatment of severe rickets caused by mutations in the vitamin D receptor (VDR) gene [GAR 01]. The known mutations in the coding regions of the human VDR gene can be divided into two classes, representing two different phenotypes. Mutations in the VDR DNA-binding domain prevent the receptor from activating gene transcription, although vitamin D binding is normal. Patients with this DNA binding defective phenotype do not respond to vitamin D treatment. In contrast, some patients with mutations in the ligand-binding domain (LBD) that cause reduced or complete hormone insensitivity are partially responsive to high doses of calcium and vitamin D, although this often necessitates long-term intravenous infusion therapy. For these patients, an alternative treatment using vitamin D analogs was proposed. Knowledge of the 3D structure of the hormone-occupied VDR LBD [ROC 00] and the nature of the amino acid residues that contribute to the functional surface of the receptor allowed the selection of three candidate VDR mutations with the potential to interact with the receptor at amino acid contact points that differ from those utilized by the natural ligand, thus restoring the function of mutant VDRs. This example clearly illustrates the importance of polymorphism data that, combined with structural and evolutionary information, can form the basis for biochemical and cellular studies, which may eventually lead to new drug therapies.

PART 2

Traditional Multiple Sequence Alignment Methods

In Part 1 of this book, we discussed how multiple alignments play a fundamental role in most of the computational methods used in genomic or proteomic projects, ranging from gene identification and the functional characterization of gene products to organism classification, genetics, human health and therapeutics. Since multiple alignments are usually employed at the beginning of the data analysis pipelines, it is crucial that the alignments are of high quality. Errors in the initial alignment will lead to further errors in the subsequent analyses and might result in false hypotheses [BLA 13]. Given the pivotal role of multiple alignments, the field has received a lot of attention and this part gives an overview of the vast array of methods developed over the years to construct multiple sequence alignments. First, in Chapter 2, we will trace the evolution of multiple alignment algorithms from their beginnings in the 1970s to the introduction of approximations or heuristics, including progressive, integrative and cooperative strategies. Chapter 3 will then discuss more formal, statistical-based approaches. Finally, Chapters 4 and 5 will be dedicated to the traditional approaches for the evaluation of the quality of multiple sequence alignments, including objective functions and alignment benchmarks.

2

Heuristic Sequence Alignment Methods

There exist two main categories of sequence alignment: pairwise alignment (or the alignment of two sequences) and multiple alignment. Pairwise alignments are most commonly used in database search programs such as Fasta [PEA 98] and Blast [ALT 97] in order to detect homologs of a novel sequence. Multiple alignments, containing from three to several thousand sequences, are more computationally complex than pairwise alignments and, in general, simultaneous alignment of more than a few sequences is rarely attempted. Instead, some sort of heuristics is generally used to reduce the search space for the multiple alignment.

The purpose of any sequence alignment, whether pairwise or multiple, is to show how a set of sequences may be related, in terms of conserved residues, substitutions, and insertion or deletion events (described in section 1.2). Multiple alignment is thus used to model relationships within a set of sequences that may have been diverging for millions of years. These relationships are typically either evolutionary, structural or functional. Unfortunately, an in-depth knowledge of the evolutionary history and structural/functional properties of the sequences is not usually available, and thus the "correct" alignment for a given set of distantly related sequences is generally not known. The most suitable solution will depend on the specific interests of the user.

This chapter describes the development of methods for the construction of sequence alignments, from the first algorithms for the "optimal" alignment of two sequences using dynamic programming, via the traditional progressive and/or iterative methods for the efficient construction of multiple alignments to the introduction of cooperative strategies that combine complementary algorithms or information other than the sequence itself.

2.1. Optimal sequence alignment

2.1.1. *Dynamic programming*

An "optimal" MSA, corresponding to the maximization of a given scoring function, can be obtained using the dynamic programming technique. Dynamic programming is a rigorous mathematical and computational method where a complicated problem is simplified by subdividing it into smaller components in a repeated manner. It is guaranteed to find the maximal scoring alignment for a set of sequences. The dynamic programming technique can be applied to global alignments by using methods such as the Needleman–Wunsch algorithm [NEE 70], and local alignments by using the Smith–Waterman algorithm [SMI 81].

The Needleman–Wunsch algorithm for the alignment of two sequences $X = x_1,\dots,x_n$ and $Y = y_1,\dots,y_m$ can be summarized as follows:

$$H_{i,j} = \text{MAX} \begin{Bmatrix} H_{i-1,j-1} + S_{i,j} \\ \text{MAX}\left(H_{i-k,j} - g - hk\right) \\ \text{MAX}\left(H_{i,j-1} - g - hl\right) \end{Bmatrix}$$

where

– $S_{i,j}$ is the score for aligning residues xi and yj;

– $H_{i,j}$ is the score of the optimal alignment of subsequences $x_1,\dots,x_i$ and $y_1,\dots,y_j$;

– g is the penalty for opening a gap;

– h is the penalty for extending a gap by one residue;

– k, l are the lengths of the gaps in sequences X and Y, respectively.

The optimal local alignment between two sequences, in which only the highest scoring subsegments are aligned, involves a simple modification to the Needleman–Wunsch method [SMI 81]. The additional constraint, $H_{ij} \geq 0$, is included in the recursive algorithm, so that the alignment can start or end at any pair of residues.

Both of these algorithms can be visualized by the construction of a two-dimensional alignment matrix of partial alignment scores (Figure 2.1).

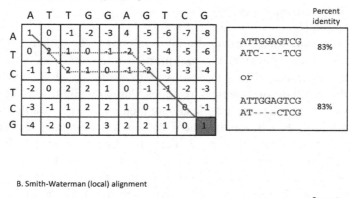

Figure 2.1. *Dynamic programming matrices for global and local alignments of two DNA sequences*

COMMENT ON FIGURE 2.1.– *Percent identity scores for each alignment are calculated by dividing the number of identical residues aligned by the total number of residues aligned.*

Each position in the matrix contains the score for the best partial alignment that ends at that position. The best scoring partial alignment can then be extended to subsequent positions in the matrix, by either aligning one residue from each sequence or by inserting a gap into one or other of the sequences. In this way, all possible alignments are considered and the final alignment is thus the best scoring alignment possible. The optimal global alignment score is given in the bottom right-hand corner of the alignment matrix, while the optimal local alignment score is defined as the highest-scoring position anywhere in the alignment matrix.

2.1.2. *Alignment parameters*

Optimal alignment methods, like most of the other methods described in this chapter, try to optimize an overall score for the multiple alignment. The simplest way to score an alignment is to count the number of identical residues that are aligned. When the sequences to be aligned are closely related, this will usually find a good solution. For more divergent sequences, however, the scores given to non-identical, but similar, residues becomes critically important. More sophisticated scoring schemes exist for both DNA and protein sequences, and generally take the form of a matrix defining the score for aligning each pair of residues. For alignments of nucleotide sequences, the simplest scoring matrix would assign the same score to a match of the four bases, ACGT, and 0 for any mismatch. However, transitions (substitution of A–G or C–T) happen much more frequently than transversions (substitution of A–T or G–C) and these substitutions are often scored differently. More complex matrices also exist in which matches between ambiguous bases are given values if there is an overlap in the sets of bases represented by the two symbols being compared. For protein sequence comparisons, scoring matrices generally take into account the biochemical similarities between amino acids and/or the relative frequencies with which each amino acid is substituted by another. Some of the most widely used scoring matrices are known as the point accepted mutation (PAM) matrices [DAY 78], an example of which is shown in Figure 2.2.

	A	R	N	D	C	Q	E	G	H	I	L	K	M	F	P	S	T	W	Y	V	B	Z	X
A	2	-2	0	0	-2	0	0	1	-1	-1	-2	-1	-1	-3	1	1	1	-6	-3	0	0	0	0
R	-2	6	0	-1	-4	1	-1	-3	2	-2	-3	3	0	-4	0	0	-1	2	-4	-2	-1	0	-1
N	0	0	2	2	-4	1	1	0	2	-2	-3	1	-2	-3	0	1	0	-4	-2	-2	2	1	0
D	0	-1	2	4	-5	2	3	1	1	-2	-4	0	-3	-6	-1	0	0	-7	-4	-2	3	3	-1
C	-2	-4	-4	-5	12	-5	-5	-3	-3	-2	-6	-5	-5	-4	-3	0	-2	-8	0	-2	-4	-5	-3
Q	0	1	1	2	-5	4	2	-1	3	-2	-2	1	-1	-5	0	-1	-1	-5	-4	-2	1	3	-1
E	0	-1	1	3	-5	2	4	0	1	-2	-3	0	-2	-5	-1	0	0	-7	-4	-2	3	3	-1
G	1	-3	0	1	-3	-1	0	5	-2	-3	-4	-2	-3	-5	0	1	0	-7	-5	-1	0	0	-1
H	-1	2	2	1	-3	3	1	-2	6	-2	-2	0	-2	-2	0	-1	-1	-3	0	-2	1	2	-1
I	-1	-2	-2	-2	-2	-2	-2	-3	-2	5	2	-2	2	1	-2	-1	0	-5	-1	4	-2	-2	-1
L	-2	-3	-3	-4	-6	-2	-3	-4	-2	2	6	-3	4	2	-3	-3	-2	-2	-1	2	-3	-3	-1
K	-1	3	1	0	-5	1	0	-2	0	-2	-3	5	0	-5	-1	0	0	-3	-4	-2	1	0	-1
M	-1	0	-2	-3	-5	-1	-2	-3	-2	2	4	0	6	0	-2	-2	-1	-4	-2	2	-2	-2	-1
F	-3	-4	-3	-6	-4	-5	-5	-5	-2	1	2	-5	0	9	-5	-3	-3	0	7	-1	-4	-5	-2
P	1	0	0	-1	-3	0	-1	0	0	-2	-3	-1	-2	-5	6	1	0	-6	-5	-1	-1	0	-1
S	1	0	1	0	0	-1	0	1	-1	-1	-3	0	-2	-3	1	2	1	-2	-3	-1	0	0	0
T	1	-1	0	0	-2	-1	0	0	-1	0	-2	0	-1	-3	0	1	3	-5	-3	0	0	-1	0
W	-6	2	-4	-7	-8	-5	-7	-7	-3	-5	-2	-3	-4	0	-6	-2	-5	17	0	-6	-5	-6	-4
Y	-3	-4	-2	-4	0	-4	-4	-5	0	-1	-1	-4	-2	7	-5	-3	-3	0	10	-2	-3	-4	-2
V	0	-2	-2	-2	-2	-2	-2	-1	-2	4	2	-2	2	-1	-1	-1	0	-6	-2	4	-2	-2	-1
B	0	-1	2	3	-4	1	3	0	1	-2	-3	1	-2	-4	-1	0	0	-5	-3	-2	3	2	-1
Z	0	0	1	3	-5	3	3	0	2	-2	-3	0	-2	-5	0	0	-1	-6	-4	-2	2	3	-1
X	0	-1	0	-1	-3	-1	-1	-1	-1	-1	-1	-1	-1	-2	-1	0	0	-4	-2	-1	-1	-1	-1

Figure 2.2. *PAM-250 substitution matrix for protein sequences*

The original PAM1 matrix was constructed based on the mutations observed in a large number of alignments of closely related sequences. A series of matrices was then extrapolated from the PAM1. The matrices range from strict matrices, useful for comparing very closely related sequences, to very "soft" matrices that are used to compare very divergent sequences. For example, the PAM250 matrix corresponds to an evolutionary distance of 250% or approximately 80% amino acid divergence. Other sets of matrices have been derived directly from either sequence-based or structure-based alignments. For example, the BLOSUM matrices [HEN 92] are based on the observed substitutions in aligned sequence segments from the Blocks database. Thus, the BLOSUM-62 matrix is based on alignment blocks in which all the sequences share at least 62% residue identity. Other more specialized matrices have been developed for specific secondary structure elements [LUT 91] or for the comparison of particular types of proteins such as transmembrane proteins [NG 00].

As well as assigning scores for residue matches and mismatches, most alignment methods calculate costs for the insertion or extension of gaps in the sequences. One of the first gap scoring schemes for the alignment of two sequences used a fixed penalty for each residue in either sequence aligned with a gap in the other. Under this system, the cost of a gap is proportional to its length. Alignment algorithms implementing such length-proportional gap penalties are efficient, however the resulting alignments often contain a large number of short insertions/deletions that are not biologically meaningful. To address this problem, linear or "affine" gap costs are used that define a "gap opening" penalty in addition to a length-dependent "gap extension" penalty. Thus, a smaller number of long gaps are favored over many short ones. Algorithms using affine gap costs are only slightly more complex than those using length-proportional gap penalties, and the space and time requirements are of the same order of magnitude. Again, more complex schemes have been developed, such as "concave" gap costs [BEN 93] or position-specific gap penalties [THO 95, WRA 04], that try to mimic the biological processes or constraints that are thought to regulate the evolution of DNA or protein sequences.

2.1.3. *Limitations*

In theory, dynamic programming approaches could be extended to more than two sequences and indeed, the first formal algorithm for multiple sequence alignment [SAN 75] was developed as a direct extension of the pairwise dynamic programming algorithm. However, in practice, it is too complex, because the time and space complexity becomes very large. For N individual sequences, the naive method requires the construction of the N-dimensional equivalent of the matrix formed in standard pairwise sequence alignment and has time complexity $O(L^N)$ for aligning N sequences of length L. The construction of the optimal global alignment for N sequences has been shown to be an NP-complete problem [WAN 94]. Consequently, more sophisticated methods are required. Some attempts have been made to perform an optimal or a suboptimal alignment within some well-defined bounds [LIP 89, STO 97]. Unfortunately, they are still limited by the number of sequences they can handle, as well as the type of objective function they can optimize.

2.2. Progressive multiple alignment

A different approach to the optimal alignment method involves the use of heuristics or "approximate" methods, which do not guarantee an optimal alignment solution, but are less time consuming than the rigorous dynamic programming techniques. Traditionally, the most popular heuristic method has been the progressive alignment procedure [FEN 87], which exploits the fact that homologous sequences are evolutionarily related. A multiple sequence alignment is built up gradually using a series of pairwise alignments, following the branching order in a phylogenetic tree. An example using five immunoglobulin-like protein domains is shown in Figure 2.3.

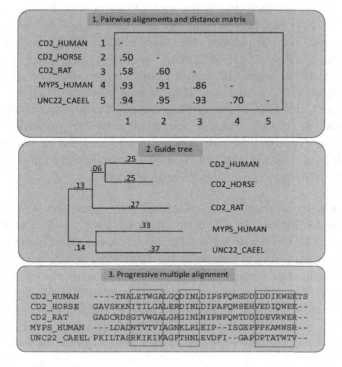

Figure 2.3. *Basic progressive alignment procedure*

COMMENT ON FIGURE 2.3.– *The algorithm is illustrated using a set of five immunoglobulin-like domains. (1) Each pair of sequences is aligned and a pairwise distance is calculated. (2) Based on the distance matrix, a guide tree is constructed. (3) All sequences are aligned together following the order in the guide tree. Secondary structure elements corresponding to CD2_HUMAN are indicated by red boxes on the MSA.*

The first step involves the comparison of all possible pairs of sequences and the calculation of some kind of pairwise distance score. Sequence pairs can be aligned using dynamic programming (see section 2.1) or a more approximate measure can be used, such as the number of shared k-mers. Based on these pairwise distances, a guide tree is then created and is used to determine the order of the multiple alignment. In general, the two closest sequences are aligned first and then larger and larger sets of sequences are merged, until all the sequences are included in the multiple alignment. In the example in Figure 2.3, the human and horse CD2 sequences are aligned first. These two sequences are then aligned with the rat CD2 sequence. Finally, MYPS_HUMAN sequence is aligned with the UNC22_CAEEL sequence, before being merged with the alignment of the three CD2 sequences. This procedure works well when the sequences to be aligned are of different degrees of divergence, since alignment of closely related sequences can be performed very accurately. By the time the more distantly related sequences are aligned, important information about the variability at each position is available from those sequences already aligned.

Most early aligners were based on the progressive method, for example Multalign [BAR 87], Multal [TAY 87], ClustalW/X [THO 94, THO 97]. The main difference between these programs lies in the algorithm used to determine the final order of alignment. Multal uses a sequential branching algorithm to identify the two closest sequences first and subsequently align the next closest sequence to those already aligned. Multalign uses a simple bottom-up data clustering method, known as the UPGMA means [SNE 73], to construct a phylogenetic tree that is then used to guide the progressive alignment step. ClustalW/X uses another phylogenetic tree construction method called neighbor joining (NJ) [GAS 97]. Although the NJ method is less efficient than the UPGMA, it has been extensively tested and usually finds a tree that is quite close to the optimal tree.

The sensitivity of the basic progressive multiple sequence alignment method has been improved by the introduction of several important enhancements. For example, ClustalW/X addresses the problem of the overrepresentation of certain sequences by incorporating a sequence weighting scheme that downweights near-duplicate sequences and upweights the most divergent ones. In addition, position-specific gap penalties are used to encourage the alignment of new gaps on existing gaps introduced earlier in the multiple alignment. In PRANK [LÖY 05], phylogenetic information from related sequences is used to distinguish between insertions and deletions, and permits the "reuse" of existing gap penalties for inserted characters without further penalty in the next stage of the progressive alignment. This strategy was shown to improve alignment quality and, in particular, the subsequent evolutionary analyses.

An alternative approach to the global multiple alignment methods described above was implemented in the DIALIGN aligner [SUB 08]. The main difference between DIALIGN and the other progressive alignment approaches is the underlying scoring scheme: instead of summing up substitution scores for aligned residues and subtracting gap penalties, the score of an alignment is based on P-values of local gap-free alignments called "segments". The segments representing locally conserved residue patterns or motifs are combined to construct a local multiple alignment of only the most conserved regions of the sequences. Thus, only those parts of the sequences that share some statistically significant similarity are included in the final multiple alignment, while unrelated parts of the sequences remain unaligned.

2.3. Iterative alignment

A major problem with the progressive approach described in section 4.2 is that the multiple alignment is constructed based on pairwise alignments and larger subsets of the sequences. Once a subset of sequences has been aligned, their alignment to each other is fixed and cannot be changed at a later stage, as more sequences are included that bring new information. In other words, errors introduced early in the multiple alignment phase cannot be rectified later as the rest of the sequences are added in.

To address this issue, the next generation of multiple alignment algorithms used iterative strategies to refine and improve the initial alignment. Iterative alignment methods use strategies that produce an initial alignment and then refine it through a series of cycles (iterations) until no more improvement can be made (convergence). Iterative methods can be deterministic or stochastic, depending on the method used to improve the alignment. In this section, we will focus on the deterministic iterative strategies, which involve extracting sequences from a multiple alignment and realigning them to the remaining sequences. Stochastic iterative methods will be discussed in Chapter 4.

One of the first attempts to use iteration techniques was implemented in the Prrp aligner [GOT 96]. An MSA is partitioned into two groups, which are then realigned using an approximate group-to-group alignment algorithm. The new MSA replaces the old one if it has a higher score. This process is repeated until no more improvements are made. In early benchmark studies [THO 99], this approach was shown to achieve higher accuracy in many alignment cases compared to the traditional progressive methods, although this was achieved with a significant time cost. Since then, other more efficient methods have been developed, including MAFFT [KAT 02], MUSCLE [EDG 04] and KALIGN [LAS 05]. These methods first perform very fast pairwise alignments, using a fast Fourier transform (for MAFFT) or using k-mer counting (for MUSCLE and KALIGN), together with a progressive multiple alignment method. Iterative strategies are then used to refine the progressive alignment. For example, MAFFT uses a strategy similar to that developed in Prrp to optimize either the weighted sum-of-pairs (WSP) objective function or a combination of WSP and a consistency-based score like COFFEE (Consistency-based Objective Function For alignmEnt Evaluation) (see Chapter 4 for a discussion of objective functions), while MUSCLE implements a tree-based partitioning algorithm for the iteration. Many of the statistics-based methods, including probabilistic methods, HMM training, simulated annealing and genetic algorithms, also use iterative strategies. These will be discussed in detail in Chapter 3.

It was shown in large-scale benchmark tests [THO 99, THO 11] that iterative algorithms generally increase the accuracy of alignments compared to progressive methods, although this improvement is often obtained at the expense of larger running time and memory requirements.

2.4. Consistency-based alignment

The iterative refinement strategies described in section 2.3 are generally used as a postprocessing step and alleviate many of the errors made during the initial progressive alignment. An alternative approach is implemented in consistency-based methods, which consider that "prevention is the best medicine". In these approaches, information from other sequences is used to improve the pairwise alignment step during a progressive alignment. Thus, the score for matching any two residues x_i and y_j in a pairwise alignment of sequences X and Y is adjusted, according to the support from other residues z_k that align to both x_i and y_j in the respective X–Z and Y–Z pairwise comparisons. The supporting pairwise alignments can be obtained from diverse sources, such as different sequence alignment algorithms, structure-based alignments, etc.

The idea of consistency was first introduced by [GOT 90] to identify "anchor points" that were used to reduce the search space for simultaneous multiple alignment. In the DIALIGN aligner [MOR 96], ungapped local alignments are first identified using segment-to-segment comparisons rather than matching of individual residues.

These local alignments are then weighted using consistency information from all sequences, and a global multiple alignment is built by combining the consistent segments. However, consistency-based alignment was really made popular with the development of a series of programs based on the COFFEE objective function [NOT 98]. The first program in this series, called T-Coffee [NOT 00], builds a library of pairwise alignments from consistent global and local pairwise alignments, which are assigned percent identity weights. Then, the score for aligning x_i and y_j is defined as the sum of the weights of all alignments in the library containing that aligned residue pair. The same approach has also been implemented in other methods dedicated to specific alignment problems, such as R-Coffee [WIL 08] for aligning non-coding RNA sequences, or PSI-Coffee [CHA 12] for aligning transmembrane proteins.

2.5. Cooperative alignment strategies

An early comparison of a number of different protein alignment methods based on the BAliBASE benchmark [THO 99] showed that no single algorithm was capable of constructing accurate alignments for all test cases. A similar observation was made in another study of RNA alignment programs [GAR 05], where algorithms incorporating structural information outperformed pure sequence-based methods for divergent sequences. Therefore, more recent developments in multiple alignment methods have tended toward attempts to try to combine the results of different aligners or to incorporate biological information other than the sequence itself.

Dedicated methods have been developed that combine primary sequence and 2D or 3D structure information, from either 3D structures or from computational predictions, to increase the accuracy of the multiple alignment construction process, such as Praline [BAW 14]. The T-Coffee aligner [NOT 00] can also incorporate information from heterogeneous data sources such as local and global alignments, structure alignments or known motifs in a progressive multiple alignment. In the case of the DbClustal program [THO 00], information obtained from the public sequence databases is used to improve the accuracy of global multiple alignments. Conserved motifs are extracted from the top sequences detected by a BlastP database search [ALT 97] using the Ballast program [PLE 00]. This local information is incorporated into a ClustalW global alignment in the form of a list of anchor points between pairs of sequences. Partial order alignment (POA) [LEE 02] and RAlign [SAM 06] use local algorithms that are suitable for multidomain proteins, which may contain repeated or shuffled elements.

An alternative approach was used in RASCAL [THO 03], which is a program designed to improve an existing multiple alignment constructed using any other aligner. It uses information from sequence clustering algorithms and residue conservation analysis [THO 01] in a two-step refinement process to detect and correct local alignment errors. Similarly, the Refiner program [CHA 06] can be used to refine a multiple sequence alignment, by iterative realignment of its individual sequences with a predetermined conserved segment (block) model of a protein family. The block model is extracted from the CDD database of conserved domain alignments [MAR 02].

Most of the methods described in this section can be used to align both protein and nucleic acid sequences. However, some methods have also been developed that take into account the specificities of RNA molecules. For example, PMComp [HOF 04] aligns RNA sequences by first computing base pairing probability matrices and then aligning the common secondary structure in order to deduce a multiple sequence alignment. Structural information has also been incorporated in existing alignment, suites to improve the accuracy of multiple non-coding RNA alignments, including MAFFT [KAT 08], R-COFFEE [WIL 08] and ProbconsRNA [DO 05].

3

Statistical Alignment Approaches

While most alignment techniques described in Chapter 2 rely abstractly on a scoring scheme that uses substitution scores and gap penalties, they do not generally include an explicit model of the evolutionary process that generated the sequence set. Statistical methods are increasingly used in bioinformatics as a way of producing a model that better describes the system behavior and of generating solutions to biological problems.

An early example of a statistical approach to biological sequence analysis was the introduction of probabilistic matrices for scoring pairwise amino acid alignments [DAY 78] (see section 3.1) in order to quantify evolutionary preferences for certain substitutions over others. More sophisticated modeling approaches have been brought gradually into sequence analysis and provide a more formal and consistent framework in which to address complex inference problems. In this chapter, we will consider the statistical methods for alignment construction that have recently been the subject of renewed interest. We will focus on three main varieties: complex evolutionary models of insertion, deletion and mutation in multiple sequences; HMMs for the construction of profile models for representing specific protein families; and stochastic optimization techniques including simulated annealing (SA) and genetic algorithms (GAs).

3.1. Probabilistic models of sequence evolution

Evolutionary models for statistical alignment provide the most explicit representation of change in biological sequences as a stochastic process. Although a probabilistic approach to alignment was suggested as far back as the mid-1980s [BIS 86], this approach remained intractable for a number of years because of the computational complexity of the problem. The first practical basis for performing pairwise alignments in a statistical framework was the model formulated by [THO 91], known as the Thorne–Kishino–Felsenstein (TKF) model, describing how one sequence may evolve into another. In this simple model, a sequence is represented as a finite string of residues separated by links. At the start of the sequence, there is an immortal link that cannot be deleted. Insertion and deletion events are then modeled as time-continuous Markov processes. Each residue can be deleted and each link can add residue-link pairs at specified rates. In addition to this birth–death process for single residue insertions and deletions, the individual residues are subject to a continuous-time substitution process.

Subsequent work on probabilistic alignment focused on extending the TKF model to arbitrary-length insertions/deletions and multiple sequences related by a tree. Although these models often suffer from a certain lack of realism, they form the basis of most statistical alignment procedures in use today. For example, several authors have coupled the TKF models with maximum-likelihood optimization methods in order to construct multiple sequence alignments [HEI 03, MIK 02, LUN 03], and the even more complex task of coestimating alignment and sequence phylogeny [HEI 90, VIN 97, FLE 05]. Nevertheless, these methods for statistical multiple alignment are computationally demanding, and full maximum likelihood approaches are limited to small trees.

An alternative approach is to integrate the TKF-like models in Bayesian analyses, with implementations including BEAST [LUN 05], Bali-Phy [SUC 06], StatAlign [NOV 08] and HandAlign [WES 12], that use Markov chain Monte Carlo to explore the joint space of alignment and phylogeny. As for the heuristic methods described in Chapter 2, attempts have also been made to include other information in the statistical alignment process, such as 3D structural information [HER 14] or suboptimal alignments generated by probabilistic sampling [KIM 14].

3.2. Profile HMM-based alignment

A second class of probabilistic modeling techniques is based on the HMM, a statistical model that is generally applicable to time series or linear sequences. An HMM architecture, known as the profile HMM, can be used to represent a multiple sequence alignment. For each column in the alignment, a "match" state models the distribution of residues allowed. An "insert" state and "delete" state at each column allow for insertion of one or more residues after the column or deletion of the column, as shown in the simple example in Figure 3.1. The advantage of this model is that it is well grounded in theory, and the insertion/deletion penalties are not arbitrary. The main disadvantage of the model is its initial requirement of a relatively large number of sequences in order to define the state transition probabilities.

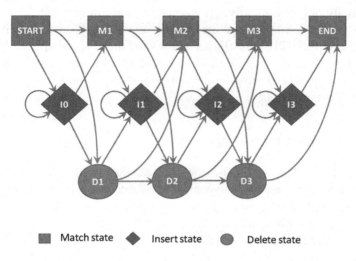

Figure 3.1. *A simple HMM example*

COMMENT ON FIGURE 3.1.– *Each state in the model represents the possibility of a match, deletion or insertion. Transition probabilities between states are represented by arrows.*

After the initial training phase, sequences can be aligned to the profile HMM and a score calculated based on the probability parameters [KRO 94]. Profile HMM methods can produce a single highest scoring output but can also generate a family of possible alignments that can then be evaluated for biological significance. This approach has been used in a number of programs, such as HMMER [EDD 98] or SAM-T99 [KAR 01] to build multiple alignments and has also been employed to create large reference databases of sequence alignments such as Pfam [FIN 15] and ProSite [SIG 13].

Some of the most popular statistical alignment methods, such as Probcons [DO 05], Probalign [ROS 06] and MSAProbs [LIU 10] incorporate HMM-derived posterior probabilities and alignment consistency scores in a progressive alignment strategy, together with an iterative refinement step. This combined approach has been shown in several benchmarking studies to produce some of the most accurate alignments for a wide range of MSA test cases, although the significant improvements are achieved at the expense of computational complexity. However, a variant of MSAProbs is available that is customized for GPGPU execution [GUD 14]. Finally, the PROMALS [PEI 07] aligner allows for more sophisticated HMM structures and the integration of external information from sequence database searches to retrieve additional homologs and local secondary structure predictions.

3.3. Simulated annealing

The flexibility and efficiency of stochastic iterative sampling techniques, such as SA, have also been exploited in the search for more accurate alignments. SA relies on an analogy with physics. The idea is to compare an optimization problem to a crystallization process, namely the cooling of a metal. The annealing method starts with raising the metal temperature to a very high level, where the crystal structure of atoms breaks down. As the temperature is lowered, the atoms tend to form the optimal crystalline structure, since this type of structure allows the physical lowest energy configuration. The analogy between annealing and optimization can be established by mapping the temperature to a control parameter or objective function. In addition, the perfect crystal corresponds to the global optimal solution to the problem.

In practice, to obtain an optimal MSA for a given set of sequences, a first alignment is randomly generated. A perturbation is then applied in a stochastic manner (shifting of an existing gap or introduction of a new one) and the resulting alignment is evaluated with an objective function [ISH 93, KIM 94]. If the new alignment is better than the previous one, it is accepted. Otherwise, it is accepted with a probability that depends on the difference between the two scores and the current temperature. At higher temperatures, a larger score difference is more likely to be accepted. If the temperature is lowered slowly enough, it can be proved that the system reaches a global optimum.

MSACSA [JOO 08] is an aligner that applies a SA method called conformational space annealing (CSA) combining SA, GAs and Monte Carlo with minimization. One of the advantages of MSACSA is that it can produce many suboptimal alignments in addition to the global optimal alignment for a given objective function. This is due to the fact that CSA can maintain conformational diversity while searching for the conformations with low energies. Unfortunately, the computational time required to reach an optimal alignment grows exponentially with the size of the alignment. To address this problem, a fast statistical alignment (FSA) aligner [BRA 09] was developed based on pair HMMs and that uses a sequence annealing algorithm to combine the posterior probabilities estimated from these models into a multiple alignment. FSA can be used to align hundreds of sequences and its explicit statistical model provides estimates of the alignment accuracy and uncertainty for every column and character of the alignment.

3.4. Genetic algorithms

GAs are stochastic search methods that mimic the metaphor of natural biological evolution, modeling natural processes, such as selection, recombination, mutation, migration, locality and neighborhood. They have been used successfully in a wide variety of applications to find solutions for hard optimization problems, including in many areas of computational biology [MAN 13]. This technique is useful for finding the optimal or near optimal solutions for combinatorial optimization problems that traditional methods fail to solve efficiently. A GA is a population-based method where each individual of the population represents a candidate solution for the target problem. This population of solutions evolves throughout several generations, in general starting from a randomly generated one. At each generation of the evolutionary process, all the individuals in the population are evaluated by a fitness function, which measures how good the solution represented by the individual is for the target problem. Selected individuals (usually those having the highest fitness) become parents and produce "offspring", i.e. new individuals that inherit some features from their parents, while others (with lower fitness) are discarded. The generation of new offspring, from the selected parents of the current generation, is accomplished by means of genetic operators. This process is iteratively repeated until a satisfactory solution is found or some stop criterion is reached, such as the maximum number of generations.

One of the first uses of GA for multiple sequence alignment was implemented in the SAGA aligner [NOT 96, NOT 97], shortly before a similar work by Zhang [ZHA 97]. In SAGA, each individual in the population is a complete multiple alignment and operators are defined that insert and shift gaps in the alignments in a random or semirandom manner. A schematic version of the general algorithm is shown in Figure 3.2. During the initialization step, a population of alignments is generated that is as diverse as possible, either randomly generated or using dynamic programming for example. The fitness of the population is evaluated by scoring each alignment with a given objective function. A new population is then created using operators, such as crossover and mutation. Crossovers generate a child alignment by combining two parent alignments and are essential for promoting the exchange of high-quality regions. The children can then be mutated, for instance by inserting or deleting a gap. Only the weakest half of the population is replaced with the new offspring while the other half is carried over to the next generation. The process terminates when an empirical criterion is reached: after a specified number of generations or when no more improvement is observed.

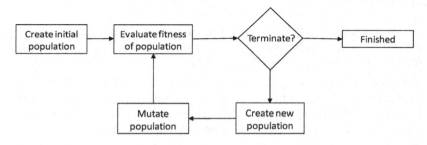

Figure 3.2. *Typical genetic algorithm for multiple sequence alignment*

Over the years, other multiple sequence alignment strategies based on GAs were introduced   [CHE 99, CAI   00]. These rely on a principle similar to SAGA, but implement better mutation operators that improve the efficiency and the accuracy of the algorithms. Shyu *et al.* [SHY 04] proposed an alternative approach, called MSA-EC, where the optimization of a consensus sequence with a GA means that the number of iterations needed to find an optimal solution is approximately the same regardless of the number of sequences being aligned. MSA-GA [GON 07] is another simple GA-based method where the initial population is generated using pairwise dynamic programming alignments. Another algorithm, GA-ant colony optimization (GA-ACO) [LEE 08], combines ACO with GA to overcome the problem of becoming trapped in local optima. To do this, at each generation of the GA, the best alignment is selected and

ACO is applied. Rubber band technique-GA (RBT-GA) [TAH 09] combines GA optimization with the RBT. RBT is inspired by the behavior of an elastic rubber band on a plate with several poles, which is analogous to locations in the input sequences that are most likely to be related. RBT is used to favor the construction of alignment columns with identical or closely related residues. In vertical decomposition with genetic algorithm (VDGA) [NAZ 11], at each generation of the GA, the sequences are divided vertically into subsequences, which are then aligned using a progressive alignment method and recombined to construct a complete multiple alignment.

More recent work has focused on improving the accuracy of GA, notably using multiobjective algorithms, such as MO-SAStrE [ORT 13], which uses eight classical MSA tools to obtain initial alignments, and three different scores are included to evaluate each alignment. The multiobjective procedure returns the subset of non-dominated alignments (Pareto front). These obtained alignments are equally good and it is not possible to decide which one is more accurate according to the three objectives. Therefore, the selection of the best alignment only depends on the objective the users consider more useful regarding the specific aligned sequences. In MSAGMOGA [KAY 14], the fitness of an individual is assessed on the basis of the number of residue matches, an affine gap penalty and a "support" score that measures the number of well-aligned sequences in the alignment. The experiments conducted on five datasets from BAliBASE showed that this approach produced high-quality results and had better efficiency than the other GA methods tested.

Many of these GA-based aligners have shown potential increases in alignment accuracy in benchmark tests, generally using small subsets of the BAliBASE benchmark. Although this clearly indicates the interest of GAs in the field of MSA, it also illustrates some of their limitations. For example, the final solutions produced may not correspond to the optimal alignment as GAs can become trapped in local optima. The results achieved can also be inconsistent, even when rerunning a GA with the same parameters, due to the stochastic nature of the process. This may be a cause of concern when using the resulting multiple alignments in downstream inference systems. GAs also suffer from another drawback: the long computational time required for useful results. Nevertheless, GA is an implicitly parallel technique, so it can be implemented very effectively on powerful parallel computers to solve large-scale problems.

4

Multiple Alignment Quality Control

Since the introduction of the first sequence alignment methods in the 1970s, a vast number of aligners have been developed that use very different algorithms, ranging from the traditional optimal dynamic programming or progressive alignment strategies or the combination of complementary techniques, such as local/global alignments or sequence/structure information (Chapter 2), to the application of statistical algorithms (Chapter 3). Although much progress has been achieved, the latest methods are still not perfect and misalignments can occur. If these misalignments are not detected, they will lead to further errors in the subsequent applications that are based on the multiple alignment (discussed in Chapter 1). The assessment of the quality and significance of a multiple alignment has therefore become a critical task, particularly in high-throughput data processing systems, where a manual verification using MSA viewers and editors, such as JalView [WAT 09] or Belvu [BAR 16], is no longer possible.

A number of quality issues can be distinguished. First, given a set of sequences, how can we evaluate the quality of a multiple alignment of those sequences? The most reliable way is probably to compare the alignment to a reference alignment, based on 3D structural superpositions for instance. In the absence of a known reference, a score can be calculated, known as an objective function, which estimates how close the alignment is to the correct or optimal solution. Thus, an objective function is the criteria used to evaluate the quality of a given alignment. To be of any use, the value that this function associates to an alignment must reflect its biological relevance and the structural or the evolutionary relations that exist among the aligned sequences. In theory, a multiple alignment is correct if the aligned residues in each column have the same evolutionary history or play similar roles in the 3D fold of the molecule. Since evolutionary or structural information is rarely available, it is common practice to replace them with a measure of sequence similarity. The rationale behind this is that similar sequences can be assumed to share the same fold and the same evolutionary origin. Objective scoring functions are discussed in section 5.1. In general, most multiple alignments contain regions that are well aligned and regions that contain errors. Section 5.2 describes methods that can distinguish reliable from unreliable regions in a multiple alignment. Finally, most multiple alignment methods available today will produce an alignment even if the sequences are unrelated. Therefore, even if the alignment is optimal, this does not mean that the sequences are actually homologous. In section 5.3, we discuss methods to estimate homology and detect unrelated sequences.

4.1. Objective scoring functions

Given a particular set of sequences, an objective score is needed that describes the optimal or "biologically correct" multiple alignment. Suboptimal or incorrect alignments would then score less than this maximal score. Such measures, also known as objective functions, are currently used to evaluate and compare multiple alignments from different sources and to detect low-quality alignments. They are also used in statistical or iterative alignment methods to improve the alignment by seeking to maximize the objective function.

One of the first scoring systems was the sum-of-pairs score [CAR 88]. For each pair of sequences in the multiple alignment, a score is calculated based on the percent identity or the similarity between the sequences. The score for the multiple alignment, $S(m)$, is then taken to be the sum of all the pairwise scores:

$$S(m) = \sum_{i<j, j<N} s(i,j)$$

where $s(i, j)$ is the score of the pairwise alignment between sequences i and j and N is the total number of sequences in the alignment.

Sequence weighting is a common modification of the traditional sum-of-pairs objective function that can be useful when the representation of sequence subfamilies in a multiple alignment is skewed. In general, overrepresented sequences are assigned lower weights, while underrepresented sequences receive higher weights.

Pairwise alignment scores are also used in the COFFEE objective function [NOT 98], which reflects the level of consistency between a multiple sequence alignment and a library containing pairwise alignments of the same sequences. This method was shown to be a good estimation of the accuracy of the multiple alignment when high-quality pairwise alignments, such as 3D structural superpositions, are available as reference. Nevertheless, one problem with multiple alignment scores based on pairwise sequence comparisons is that they assume that substitution probabilities are uniform at all positions in the alignment. This is unrealistic as some positions will be more variable than others depending on the functional or structural constraints of the molecule.

For this reason, some authors have introduced objective functions based on column statistics. One approach uses information content, assuming that the most interesting alignments are those where the frequencies of the residues found in each column are significantly different from a predefined set of *a priori* residue probabilities [HER 99]. The information content of a multiple alignment is defined as:

$$I(m) = \sum_{j=1}^{L} \sum_{i=1}^{A} f_{i,j} \ln \frac{f_{i,j}}{p_i}$$

where $f_{i,j} = \dfrac{n_{i,j}}{N}$ is the frequency that residue i occurs at position j, $n_{i,j}$ is the frequency that residue i occurs at position j, N is the total number of sequences in the alignment, A is the size of the alphabet, L is the total number of positions in the alignment, p_i is the *a priori* probability of residue i.

One disadvantage of this measure is that it considers only the frequencies of identical residues in each column and does not take into account similarities between residues. Therefore, another column-based measure, norMD, was introduced [THO 01], based on the mean distance (MD) column scores implemented in ClustalX [THO 97]. A score for each column in the alignment is calculated based on the mean pairwise distance between sequences in a continuous sequence space, and the column scores are summed over the full length of the alignment. The total score is then normalized to take into account the number, length and similarity of the sequences in the alignment, and the presence of gaps.

An evaluation of several different objective functions was performed using the reference multiple alignments in the BAliBASE benchmark database (described in Chapter 5). It was shown that the sum-of-pairs score increases proportionally with the number of the sequences in the alignment. Thus, an alignment containing many sequences will score higher than an alignment of fewer sequences, regardless of the respective quality. The information content measure solves the problem of the number of sequences, as all columns will score between 0 and 1. However, the scores increase proportionally with the length of the alignment. The norMD score partially resolves these problems and can be used to estimate the quality of the alignment even when the optimal alignment score is unknown. Using norMD, most of the alignments scoring higher than the threshold score of 0.5 were correct, while alignments scoring less than 0.3 were generally of poor quality. Nevertheless, a twilight zone still exists for norMD scores between 0.3 and 0.5, where no distinction can be made between good and bad alignments.

4.2. Determination of reliable regions

The objective functions described above calculate a global score that estimates the overall quality of a multiple alignment. However, even when misalignments occur, it is not necessarily true that all of the alignment is incorrect. Useful information could still be extracted if the reliable regions in the alignment are distinguished from the unreliable regions. The prediction of the reliability of specific alignment positions has therefore been an area of much interest. One of the first automatic methods for the analysis of local conservation in protein sequence alignments was the AMAS program [LIV 93], which used a set-based description of amino acid properties. Since then, a large number of different methods have been proposed. For example, Al2Co [PEI 01] calculates a conservation index at each position in a multiple sequence alignment using weighted residue frequencies at each position. The DIVAA method [ROD 04] is based on a statistical measure of the diversity at a given position and is also used for protein sequence alignments. If the position is completely conserved (i.e. only one amino acid is observed in all the sequences analyzed), the diversity is 0.05 (1/20); if it contains equal proportions of all amino acids, the diversity is 1.0 (20/20). Diversity as defined here is inversely and nonlinearly related to the measure of sequence information content described above, with a highly conserved position exhibiting relatively low diversity and high information content. For nucleic acid sequences, the ConFind program [SMA 05] identifies regions of conservation in multiple sequence alignments that can serve as diagnostic targets and is designed to work with a large number of highly mutable target sequences such as viral genomes. ConFind attempts to calculate the entropy score (equivalent to the information content score defined above) for each alignment column, assigning either a bit score or "none" for columns with an insufficient number of non-ambiguous characters.

An alternative approach for identifying reliable regions in an MSA has been implemented recently in the MUMSA program [LAS 05] based on the comparison of several alignments of the same sequences.

The idea is to search for regions that are identically aligned in many alignments, assuming that these are more reliable than regions differently aligned in many alignments. The method also results in a score for a given alignment. In this case, a high-quality alignment is one that shares more aligned residues with other alignments. The choice of multiple alignment methods used as input is therefore crucial in order to avoid a bias toward one particular algorithm. Ideally, different algorithms should be used, such as local and global methods, algorithms designed for transmembrane sequences, repeats, etc. A similar concept is implemented in heads or tails (HoT) [LAN 07], which compares an MSA and its flipped version (where the sequences are in reversed order) obtained through the same aligner to identify the most reliable portions inside an MSA. This concept was recently taken a bit further in GUIDANCE [PEN 10], which uses alternative guide trees obtained from bootstrap replicates to estimate alternative MSAs and turn their consistency into a reliability index. An extended version of the pairwise library-based COFFEE objective function, called transitive consistency score (TCS) [CHA 14], has also been developed to identify the most reliable portions of an MSA and was shown notably to improve subsequent phylogenetic tree reconstruction based on the filtered alignments. Based on benchmarking experiments with structure-based datasets, these more complex methods were shown to outperform the simpler scores. However, a major drawback is that several alignments of the same sequences have to be constructed for the purpose of comparison, which is not always computationally feasible.

An alternative approach to the calculation of position conservation scores is to use a graphical representation for displaying the patterns in a set of aligned sequences, known as sequence logos, first introduced in 1990 [SCH 90]. Figure 4.1 shows an example display created using the WebLogo server [CRO 04]. The characters representing the sequence are stacked on top of each other for each position in the aligned sequences. The height of each letter is proportional to its frequency, and the letters are sorted so the most common one is on top. The height of the entire stack is then adjusted to indicate the information content of the sequences at that position.

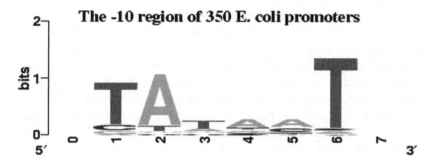

Figure 4.1. *An example of sequence logo for displaying patterns in aligned sequences. For a color version of the figure, see www.iste.co.uk/thompson/statistics.zip*

COMMENT ON FIGURE 4.1.– *The logo represents a conserved region, known as the Pribnow box, found upstream of the transcription start point in prokaryotic genomes.*

The frequency-based measures were replaced recently by a more formal statistical approach for sequences logos, using normalized maximum likelihood and Bayesian measures of column information [YU 14].

4.3. Estimation of homology

An important aspect of sequence alignment is to establish how meaningful a given alignment is. It is always possible to construct an alignment between a set of sequences, even if they are unrelated. The problem is to determine the level of similarity required to infer that the sequences are homologous, i.e. that they descend from a common ancestor. A simple rule-of-thumb for protein sequences states that if two sequences share more than 25% identity over more than 100 residues, then the two sequences can be assumed to be homologous.

However, many proteins sharing less than 25% residue identity, said to be in the "twilight zone" [DOO 86], do still have very similar structures for example.

As seen in Chapter 1, many applications have been developed that predict or propagate biological information between the sequences in a multiple alignment based on a presumed homology. The hypothesis is that homologous sequences, i.e. sequences that have descended from the same ancestor, often share the same structure and function. A fundamental step in these so-called "homology-based" methods is the determination of the extent of similarity between the aligned sequences. Without this initial crucial step, the subsequent applications that rely on an accurate multiple alignment cannot be expected to yield high-quality results.

This particular problem has been addressed by a number of groups. Measuring the percent identity or similarity of the sequences is generally not sensitive enough to distinguish between alignments of related and unrelated sequences. Much work has been done on the significance of both ungapped and gapped pairwise local alignments [ALT 96, PEA 98], although the statistics of global alignments or alignments of more than two sequences are far less well understood. The aim of the statistical analysis is to estimate the probability of finding by "chance" at least one pairwise alignment that scores as high as or greater than the given alignment. For ungapped local alignments, these probabilities or P-values may be derived analytically. For local alignments with gaps, empirical estimates are used based on the scores obtained during a database search, or from randomly generated sequences.

The degree to which the sequences in a multiple alignment are related is a more complex problem. Some recent methods, such as LEON-BIS [VAN 16], have been developed to determine the extent of homology between proteins based on the MSA. In LEON-BIS, sequences are clustered into subfamilies and homology relations are predicted at different levels, including "core blocks", "regions" and full-length proteins, based on a formal Bayesian framework.

LEON-BIS can be used to identify the complex relationships between large multidomain proteins and should thus be useful for automatic high-throughput annotation pipelines. Another recent method, OD-seq [JEH 15], is designed to find outlier sequences in multiple sequence alignments by examining the average distance of each sequence to the rest. It is designed to provide a useful, fast method for checking very large alignments containing thousands of sequences.

5

Benchmarking

In Chapters 2 and 3, we discussed the vast array of aligners that have been developed based on diverse algorithms, or a combination of complementary techniques, and the progress achieved. When new methods are introduced, it is important to objectively measure the quality of the alignments produced by the program, and to quantify the improvement obtained compared to existing methods. Ideally, a detailed evaluation should be performed to determine the performance of the different methods under various conditions. Such studies would allow the selection of the most appropriate aligner for a given alignment problem. In-depth analyses of the strengths and weaknesses of the different aligners would also indicate guidelines for improvement of alignment algorithms.

In computer science, the quality of an algorithm is often demonstrated by comparing the results obtained with a standard benchmark, consisting of a set of tests used to measure the relative performance of different programs. The resulting evaluations indicate where the programs need to be improved and what new features need to be incorporated with the aim of increasing specific aspects of performance. Thus, the creation and acceptance of a benchmark within a field often results in a stronger consensus within the community, more rigorous examination of algorithm results, and faster technical progress [ANI 10]. In section 5.1, we will consider the criteria to be taken into account when building or using a benchmark. We will then present some of the most widely used benchmarks for MSA in section 5.2, and in section 5.3, we will compare their applicability in specific situations.

5.1. Criteria for benchmark construction

There are three main issues involved in the definition of a MSA benchmark. First, how many test cases are needed and which sequences should be included in the tests? Second, how should the "correct" alignment of the sequences be determined? Third, how should the alignment produced by a program be compared with the benchmark alignment?

5.1.1. *Defining the benchmark test cases*

In general, it is not necessary (or possible) to include all possible alignments in a benchmark and it is sufficient to provide enough representative tests in order to calculate statistical significance and to differentiate between the different methods tested. One way of producing large numbers of sequences is to simulate evolutionary processes and create sets of artificial sequences with known homology relations. Because of high-throughput genome sequencing of numerous organisms, there are also huge numbers of real DNA, RNA and protein sequences available in public databases, such as RefSeq or UniProtKB. In the case of a MSA benchmark based on 3D structure comparisons, the largest source of protein structures is the PDB database [KOU 06], although this set contains a certain amount of bias due to overrepresented structures. However, the difficulty of an MSA problem also depends on the nature of the set of sequences to be aligned. Therefore, the benchmark alignments should also include example test cases representing the diverse problems encountered when performing multiple alignments, such as different numbers of sequences and different sequence diversity or sequence length.

5.1.2. Defining the correct alignment

The goal of a multiple sequence alignment is to identify equivalent residues in nucleic acid or protein molecules that have evolved from a common ancestor. However, the true evolutionary history cannot usually be reconstructed and therefore, the "correctness" of an alignment has been measured based on different strategies [IAN 14]. These include simulated sequences where the homology relations are known, consistency between different alignment methods, phylogeny-based assessments, or more commonly comparison with 3D structure superpositions. In general, the 3D structure of an RNA or protein is more conserved than the sequence and a structural superposition can thus provide an objective reference alignment [KOE 02]. Although there are inherent ambiguities in deriving a sequence alignment from structure superpositions, most algorithms are in agreement for the more conserved regions. Consequently, many structure-based multiple alignment benchmarks define reliable regions or 'blocks' in the alignments, where the sequences are assumed to be correctly aligned.

5.1.3. Defining the alignment score

In addition to the alignment test cases, a benchmark should also include a means of comparing a test alignment with the benchmark alignment. Most MSA benchmarks use either the SP score, defined here as the percentage of pairwise residues aligned the same in both alignments, or the percentage of complete columns aligned the same. Recently, a new alignment benchmark scoring scheme has been proposed, called SPdist [BAW 15], that takes the degree of discordance of mismatches into account by measuring the sequence distance between mismatched residue pairs in the query alignment. In tests using the BAliBASE benchmark [THO 05], it was shown that for more divergent alignments, the SPdist score was able to distinguish between methods that produce alignments close to the reference alignment, and those that exhibit larger shifts. The most appropriate score will depend on the sequences in the benchmark test case and the subsequent applications of the MSA, and it may be appropriate to explore different scores to study the alignment quality of alternative MSAs.

5.2. Multiple alignment benchmarks

One of the first studies to compare the quality of different aligners [MCC 94] used four sets of sequences from the hemoglobin, kinase, aspartic acid protease and ribonuclease H protein families. Several progressive aligners, including both global and local methods, were compared, and alignment quality was estimated by the number of highly conserved motifs identified. They concluded that in general global methods performed better than local methods. However, the number of suitable sequences available at that time was limited and this was therefore not a comprehensive test. Since then, a number of larger, more comprehensive benchmark test sets have been developed. These benchmarks are used to compare and evaluate the different aligners, to select the most suitable aligner for a given set of sequences (e.g. more efficient, more correct, more scalable), to quantify the improvements obtained when new aligners are introduced and to identify the strong and weak points of the different algorithms. In the following sections, we will describe some of the more widely used benchmark sets.

5.2.1. BAliBASE

BAliBASE [THO 99] was one of the first large-scale benchmarks specifically designed for multiple alignment of protein sequences. The test cases in BAliBASE are based on 3D structural superpositions that are manually refined to ensure the correct alignment of functional residues. Although the expert refinement process means that the alignments are of high quality, one drawback of this approach is that the test cases are necessarily limited in size. The alignments are organized into reference sets that represent real MSA problems, such as very divergent sequences, or sequences with large N/C-terminal extensions or internal insertions. Core blocks are defined in each alignment that exclude the regions for which the 3D structure is unreliable, for example the borders of secondary structure elements or in loop regions.

Recently, a new reference set was designed [THO 11] to overcome some of the biases inherent in structure-based benchmarks, and to represent typical problems encountered when aligning the large protein sequence sets that result from today's high throughput biotechnological methods. The new reference set thus includes multidomain architectures, transmembrane regions and natively disordered regions. Another important feature is the annotation of the core blocks that are conserved in subsets of the sequences, which often represent functional specificities of the protein subfamilies. A study using this benchmark showed that aligners have significantly progressed, and can now identify most of the shared sequence features that determine the broad molecular function(s) of a protein family, even for divergent sequences. However, a number of important challenges were highlighted. First, the locally conserved regions, which reflect functional specificities or that modulate a protein's function in a given cellular context, are less well aligned. Second, motifs in natively disordered regions are often misaligned. Third, the badly predicted or fragmentary protein sequences, which make up a large proportion of today's databases, lead to a significant number of alignment errors.

5.2.2. OxBench

The OXBench benchmark suite [RAG 03] contains multiple alignments of protein domains that are built automatically using both structure and sequence alignment methods. The test cases were selected from the 3Dee database of structural domains. From the complete 3Dee data set, 1,168 domains in 218 families were selected, such that no two sequences in a family shared ≥98% identity, and reliable regions, known as structurally conserved regions, were defined. The benchmark was then divided into three datasets. The master set contains only sequences of known 3D structure, and currently consists of 672 alignments, with from 2 to 122 sequences in each alignment. The extended dataset was then constructed by including sequences of unknown structure. Finally, the full-length dataset was built by including the full-length sequences corresponding to the domains in the master dataset.

A number of different scores are included in the benchmark suite in order to evaluate the accuracy of multiple alignment programs. Notably, the position shift error measures the average magnitude of error, so that misalignments that cause a small shift between two sequences are penalized less than large shifts. Two other measures are also provided that are independent of the reference alignment. To calculate these, the structure superposition implied by the test alignment is inferred and the quality of the test alignment is then estimated by computing the root mean square deviation of the superposition.

5.2.3. PREFAB

The PREFAB [EDG 04] benchmark was constructed using a fully automatic protocol and currently contains 1,932 multiple alignments of protein sequences. Pairs of sequences from the PDB database were selected and aligned using two different 3D structure superposition methods. Each sequence in the aligned pair was then used to query a sequence database using PSI-BLAST [ALT 97], and high-scoring hits were collected. Finally, the queries and their hits were combined to make test sets consisting of 50 sequences with an average length of 240 amino acids.

The accuracy of an alignment program is estimated based on the alignment of the structure pair in the test multiple alignment with the reference superposition in each test case. Only positions that are aligned the same by the two different superposition methods are considered. The quality of a multiple alignment program is thus evaluated by calculating the percentage of these positions that are correctly aligned in the multiple alignment.

5.2.4. SABmark

SABmark [VAN 05] contains reference sets of sequences derived from the SCOP protein structure classification, divided into two sets, twilight zone (Blast E-value $\geq$ 1) and superfamilies (residue identity $\leq$ 50%). For each test case, structure-based alignments are constructed for all pairs of sequences. However, these pairwise sequence alignments are not necessarily consistent with each other, and consequently, no unique multiple alignment solution can be constructed. Instead, in order to evaluate the quality of a multiple alignment program, multiple alignments of each test case are constructed and pairwise alignments are then extracted from the multiple alignment and compared to the reference structure superpositions.

A unique feature of SABmark are the test cases that include "false positive" sequences that are structurally unrelated to the original family members. In these sets, each group of N sequences is expanded with at most N other, structurally unrelated yet apparently similar sequences. Two different scores are provided to measure the quality of the alignment program. The first score is similar to the SP score and is defined as the ratio of the number of correctly aligned residues divided by the length of the reference alignment, and may be thought of as a measure of sensitivity. The second score measures the specificity and is defined as the ratio of the number of correctly aligned residues divided by the length of the test alignment.

5.2.5. BRAliBASE

All the above benchmarks contain protein sequence alignment test sets. However, MSAs are also essential for RNA studies, including RNA structure analysis, RNA homology search, ncRNA detection and RNA-based phylogenetic inference. BRAliBASE [GAR 05] is a benchmark specifically designed to evaluate and compare aligners on RNA datasets. It includes four diverse structural RNA datasets of Group II introns, 5S rRNA, tRNA and U5 spliceosomal RNA, obtained from the Rfam database. Approximately 100 subalignments were generated for each of the four families, containing five sequences each. This dataset was then divided into high ($\geq$75% sequence identity), medium (55–75% sequence identity) and low (<55% sequence identity) groups. An additional tRNA dataset was also generated with just two sequences in each alignment.

In order to evaluate alignment methods on structural RNAs, two quality measures are provided. The first is the traditional SP score employed in many of the protein alignment benchmarks. The second measure, known as the structure conservation index, provides an estimate of the conserved secondary structure information contained within the alignment.

5.2.6. Phylogeny-based benchmark

An alternative to the structure-based benchmarks described above involves the construction of a phylogenetic tree, based on the MSA produced by the different alignment methods. This approach is based on the assumption that more accurate alignments will produce more accurate trees. The problem then is to assess the quality of the constructed trees. In [DES 10], two methods were proposed. The first uses "species-tree discordance" and compares alignments of orthologous genes from species whose phylogeny is known. The second method, called the "minimum duplication test", is based on the parsimony of trees built from alignments of both orthologous and paralogous sequences. Trees that require fewer gene duplications to explain the data are more likely to reflect the true evolutionary history of the sequences and have higher quality scores.

The authors constructed over 100,000 test sets with up to 60 sequences each. For the species-tree discordance test, six sequences were selected from a large range of organisms, where the branching orders of the species in each set were well defined. For the minimum duplication test, sets of up to 60 sequences were constructed from different metazoan and fungal species. Trees were then reconstructed using a maximum likelihood (ML) method from both amino acid and nucleotide alignments. In addition, ML trees were also reconstructed from back-translated amino acid alignments, using the actual codons from the corresponding nucleotide sequences.

These test sets were used to evaluate 13 different aligners. The results showed that (i) consistency-based alignment methods, which score best in structural benchmarks, do not yield significantly better trees than scoring matrix-based methods; (ii) regions with gaps carry substantial phylogenetic signal, but are poorly exploited by most alignment and tree reconstruction programs; (iii) disagreement among alignment programs did not always reflect the accuracy of the resulting trees.

5.3. Comparison of multiple alignment benchmarks

The goal of an alignment benchmark is not to provide a comprehensive database of all possible alignments, but it should include sufficient test cases in order to differentiate between the different aligners being compared. All of the benchmarks described above have large numbers of alignments and have been used in a number of studies to demonstrate the relative accuracy of various alignment methods. SABmark has the largest number of test cases and boasts full coverage of the known fold space. However, there are only pairwise references for each sequence group, and measuring multiple alignment accuracy is difficult.

In addition, a comprehensive MSA benchmark should also include test cases that reproduce real-world alignment problems. Most of the benchmarks described above contain real protein or RNA sequences, except IRMBASE, which contains artificial sequences created by the authors. Many of the benchmarks are organized into a number of test sets according to the similarity of the sequences, which is clearly a major factor affecting the accuracy of a multiple alignment. Nevertheless, other characteristics of the sequences also influence the final alignment quality, including their lengths, their phylogenetic distribution, the presence of non-homologous regions or a nonlinear domain organization. A comprehensive benchmark should specifically address these diverse, complex issues.

In a comparison of a number of benchmarks for protein aligners [BLA 06], the authors demonstrated that categorizing HOMSTRAD, OxBench and PREFAB test cases by percent sequence identity yielded similar results when ranking alignment programs, as might be expected. Each of these datasets showed that the ability to accurately align sequences is largely dependent on the diversity of the sequences. OxBench, PREFAB and BAliBASE all contain difficult cases containing full-length sequences of low sequence identity. BAliBASE has the additional advantage that several distinct problem areas are explicitly addressed, which also makes the benchmark more difficult to overtrain on. Therefore, they proposed that it would be advantageous to use several benchmarks for program assessment.

In conclusion, benchmarking can highlight the strong and weak points of multiple alignment methods and has had a positive effect on the development of new alignment methodologies. Considerable effort has been applied to the development of benchmarks aimed at different aspects of the multiple alignment problem. Most of the traditional benchmarks have been designed to evaluate alignment quality, although some recent work has addressed the efficiency and scalability issues for very large sequence sets. These dedicated large-scale benchmarks will be discussed in sections 6.6 and 7.4. It should be noted that the criteria for selection of an aligner are often more complex, taking into account ease-of-use, efficiency, stability, robustness, etc. in addition to alignment accuracy and efficiency.

PART 3

Large-scale Multiple Sequence Alignment Methods

In the past 20 years, genome sequencing and assembly techniques have led to an explosion in the amount of sequence data available in public databases. The first free-living organism to be sequenced was that of *Haemophilus influenzae* (1.8 Mb) in 1995, and since then genomes have been sequenced at an ever-increasing pace. Since the human genome was completed by the Human Genome Project in 2004, extraordinary progress has been made in genome sequencing and the latest high-throughput technologies, known as NGS, have parallelized the sequencing process, producing thousands or millions of sequences concurrently. This has led to decreased costs and a huge increase in the number and diversity of sequenced genomes [GOO 16]. At the time of writing, the Genomes Online Database (www.genomesonline.org) contained genome sequence data for more than 80,000 organisms, including >13,000 eukaryotic species and >60,000 bacteria. Many of these are model organisms that occupy strategic positions in the tree of life and provide important information for evolutionary studies [BUR 14]. Other genomes have been sequenced because they have important industrial implications, such as the investigation of genetic variations in humans and their roles in health and disease [RAB 16], or the design and production of new crops, biofuels, etc. [KIM 16].

On-going large-scale sequencing projects, such as the 1000 Genomes Project (www.1000genomes.org) or the Genome 10K Project (genome10k.soe.ucsc.edu), will further transform the data landscape in the biological and medical sciences. As a result, the bottleneck to gaining new knowledge in this field is no longer data collection, but data analysis. As in other domains, biological "big data" can be defined as data whose scale, diversity and complexity require new architectures, techniques, algorithms and analytics to manage it and extract value and hidden knowledge from it. In the field of multiple sequence alignment, the large protein families produced by NGS are often complex, with multidomain architectures, long unstructured (natively disordered) regions, splicing variants, etc. In addition, the new sequences are mostly predicted by automatic methods and contain many sequence errors. The rest of this book is dedicated to the new approaches developed to respond to the challenges of these new data.

6

Whole Genome Alignment

The methods described in the earlier parts of this book were generally developed to align sets of relatively short protein or RNA sequences. However, the availability of whole genome sequences has led to an interest in MSAs for complete genomes, often referred to as whole genome alignment (WGA). In this case, specialized alignment tools are needed. The first problem concerns the increased sequence lengths: single gene sequences may be as long as tens of thousands of nucleotides, but whole genomes are usually millions of nucleotides or larger. Apart from the increased size of the data, WGA methods also need to take into account more complex evolutionary events including genome rearrangements (inversions, translocations, chromosome fusions or fissions, etc.), in addition to substitutions and insertions/ deletions. Some tools for WGA are also capable of modeling unbalanced rearrangements that lead to copy number changes, such as tandem and segmental duplications.

It is important to note that, as in the case of protein sequences, the correct alignment of whole genomes is not generally equivalent to an optimal alignment that maximizes a given scoring function [GUS 97]. Instead, it is a biological problem where homologous bases should be aligned to each other in order to identify the potentially functional sequences, such as conserved non-coding regions in introns and intergenic regions, exons in orthologous genes or groups of orthologous genes that form larger blocks of homology.

For closely related organisms, a global alignment of complete genomes may be possible since most regions will be homologous. Although even for very close genomes, inversions, repeats, etc. can be observed. For more divergent genomes, the strongly conserved regions that represent functional elements are believed to account for only a small fraction of all bases. For example, functional regions are believed to account for only about 5% of bases in mammalian genomes. Nevertheless, the conserved segments often indicate purifying selection within a genomic region and an evolutionarily conserved function. Therefore, significant efforts have been made in the field of comparative genomics to accurately locate conserved regions in a set of genomes, playing an important role in predicting novel genes and correcting previous gene structures, as well as revealing other conserved elements that do not code for proteins.

In this chapter, we will first introduce the methods for the alignment of two whole genomes, since they provide the basis for most of the multiple genome alignment methods. Different approaches for the construction of multiple WGA will then be described, as well as approaches for estimating the accuracy of the resulting alignments and benchmarking the methods.

6.1. Pairwise genome alignment

Local alignment is perhaps the most straightforward way to compare two very long sequences. Local alignment aims to find all subsequences that are shared by the two sequences with a similarity higher than a given threshold. This approach works reasonably well for finding all pairs of genes or evolutionarily constrained elements, transposons and other repeats, etc. Local similarity searches are also more robust to rearrangements between genomes, such as inversions, translocations or duplications. Therefore, the most widely used bioinformatics tools in comparative genomics have been local aligners, such as BLASTZ [ALT 97], PatternHunter [MA 02] or CHAOS [PÖH 05].

The concept of local alignment can then be extended to that of synteny blocks (also called orthology maps), which are defined as regions of conservation of orthologous gene order within two sets of chromosomes that are being compared with each other. Many tools exist for synteny/orthology mapping, including DRIMM-Synteny [PEV 03], Mercator [DEW 07], SyntenyTracker [DON 09], SynChro [DRI 14] or SynFind [TAN 15], to name but a few. They are generally based on the idea of first obtaining a set of local alignments between two genomes, and then grouping those alignments into clusters so that each cluster spans a specific region of a chromosome in each species.

Local alignments can also be used as "anchors" for global alignment methods in order to reduce the alignment search space needed for WGA (Figure 6.1). Most of these methods are based on a chaining strategy of first finding and chaining words or local alignments between two sequences, thus creating a set of anchors. These anchors effectively cut a large alignment problem into many smaller ones. The global alignment thus consists of three steps. First, exact word matching or indexes are used to find local alignments. Then, an optimal chain of local hits is constructed to create synteny blocks. Finally, the regions in between the chained blocks are aligned, which represent much smaller alignment problems.

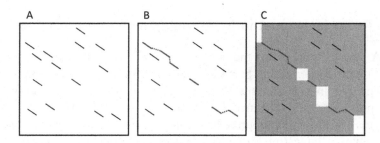

Figure 6.1. *Strategy for global alignment of long genome sequences, visualized as a dot plot For a color version of the figure, see www.iste.co.uk/thompson/statistics.zip*

COMMENT ON FIGURE 6.1.– *Two sequences are mapped along the vertical and horizontal axes. (A) Diagonal lines indicate local alignments that have similarity higher than a certain threshold (for simplicity, only subsequences aligned in the forward direction are shown). (B) Local alignments are chained to form "synteny blocks", shown in red. (C) The global alignment is restricted to the segments between the defined synteny blocks, shown as white boxes, thus excluding most of the search space (gray background).*

One of the first methods to use this approach for WGA was MUMmer [DEL 99] and could be used for efficient alignment of large-scale DNA sequences in the order of millions of nucleotides. However, the system still required relatively large amounts of time and memory, making it necessary to use powerful server computers to align larger genomes. To address this problem, the AVID program [BRA 03] used suffix trees to find all matching subsequences. These local matching subsequences were then combined as described above to create a global alignment. AVID also had the ability to align a draft sequence consisting of multiple contigs to a finished genome. Both of these methods assume that the sequences are closely related. In contrast, Limited Area Global Alignment of Nucleotides (LAGAN) [BRU 03] can be used for genomic comparisons of more distantly related organisms. This is achieved through the CHAOS algorithm, a local alignment method that detects short inexact words rather than longer exact words.

6.2. Progressive methods for multiple genome alignment

A simple strategy for the construction of a multiple whole-genome alignment is to combine pairwise local alignments, for example using the progressive alignment strategy (see section 3.2 for details of the progressive algorithm). For instance, MAVID [BRA 03] is a progressive alignment approach that incorporates maximum likelihood inference of ancestral sequences, automatic guide tree construction, protein-based anchoring of *ab initio* gene predictions and constraints derived from a global homology map of the sequences. MLAGAN [BRU 03] is another method for large-scale multiple alignment based on a progressive LAGAN alignment step, where pairwise alignments are combined in the order given by a phylogenetic tree input by the user. These methods assume that the input sequences do not have significant rearrangements of sequence elements, and select a single collinear set of alignment anchors.

Mauve [DAR 04] is a genome comparison method that identifies conserved genomic regions, rearrangements and inversions in conserved regions and the exact sequence breakpoints of such rearrangements across multiple genomes. Like the other genome alignment methods, Mauve uses anchoring as a heuristic to improve the calculation time of the alignment. Unlike other multiple genome alignment systems, Mauve does not assume that the genomes under study are collinear. Instead, Mauve identifies and aligns regions of local collinearity called locally collinear blocks (LCBs). Each LCB is a homologous sequence region shared by two or more of the genomes under study and does not contain any rearrangements. Rearrangements are only allowed between two LCBs. The method was later extended to align regions that are conserved in only a subset of the genomes [DAR 10].

Another strategy for multiple WGA was proposed in threaded-blockset aligner (TBA) [BLA 04], which constructs a "threaded blockset" of a set of genomes. A threaded blockset is defined as a set of multiple alignments (or blocks) of collinear subsequences, where each position in the input sequences is included in exactly one block. Blocks are allowed to have just one sequence in cases where the sequence is not found to have any homologs. For three or more sequences, the program MULTIZ (a component of TBA) uses dynamic programming to align the blocksets.

6.3. Graph-based methods for multiple genome alignment

In order to take into account inverted or repeated elements, a genome alignment can be represented as a directed graph, possibly containing cycles. In this context, a generalization of de Bruijn graphs has been introduced, called A-Bruijn graphs. A-Bruijn graphs have one vertex for sets of aligned positions, and edges represent sequence adjacencies. For the purpose of genome alignment with A-Bruijn graphs, the maximum subgraph with large girth problem [RAP 04] and the sequence modification problem [PHA 10] were proposed, both targeting types of short cycles in A-Bruijn graphs in order to eliminate local alignments that hide local collinearity. Two other programs, Enredo and Pecan [PAT 08], have been published that use another form of graph, called the Enredo graph. Enredo first partitions genomes into segments using Enredo graphs. Then, Pecan constructs collinear alignments of segments. Enredo graphs have two vertices per set of aligned segments, a head and a tail vertex, that are similar to breakpoint graphs used in rearrangement studies. The Enredo method iteratively eliminates various substructures from the Enredo graph before deriving a final genome segmentation. Another recent graph used for WGA is the cactus graph [PAT 11]. In cactus graphs, sequence adjacencies are represented by vertices and genome segments by edges. The structure of the cactus graph has two interesting advantages: first, the graph can be subdivided into independent units by ensuring that any edge is part of at most one simple cycle and second, a Eulerian circuit exists that traverses all genome segments exactly once, thus providing a consensus genome.

Mugsy [ANG 11] performs WGAs of draft or finished genomes in single or multiple contiguous sequences. This makes it suitable for use in *de novo* sequencing projects where a suitable closely related reference genome is not available. Mugsy uses the Nucmer algorithm, a graph-based segmentation procedure for identifying collinear regions in two genomes and a component of the MUMmer suite. Each pairwise alignment is then checked to identify orthologous matches, which excludes matches found in repetitive and duplicated sequences. Finally, the segment-based progressive alignment strategy from the TCoffee package is used to construct a multiple alignment.

6.4. Meta-aligners for multiple genome alignment

Although a number of algorithms for WGA have been developed, the alignments produced are still error-prone. Therefore, meta-methods have been described that combine the advantages of the different approaches to try to improve the reliability of the results.

For example, Crumble and Prune [ROS 11] can be used to break a global alignment problem into smaller, more tractable subproblems. These methods are complementary: while Crumble breaks long alignment problems into shorter subproblems, Prune divides the phylogenetic tree into a collection of smaller trees to reduce the number of sequences in each alignment problem. The subproblems can be solved independently, using any existing multiple sequence alignment method. The individual results are then combined to form a global solution to the full alignment problem. Experiments using simulated sequences showed that both approaches significantly reduce the time required to construct large-scale alignments, with little or no loss of accuracy.

Another meta-aligner, Robusta (www.tcoffee.org/Projects/robusta), can be used to combine different pairwise or multiple alignments from different WGA programs into a single final alignment. A typical usage of Robusta would be to cut the genomes to align them into a set of collinear homologous blocks using Mercator. These blocks are then aligned and turned into T-Coffee libraries [NOT 00]. As a final step, the T-Coffee program is used to produce an alignment for each block.

An alternative approach was developed in the Probabilistic Sampling-based Alignment Reliability-Align (PSAR-Align) realignment tool [KIM 14]. It can be used to refine an initial MSA constructed using any WGA method based on a probabilistic framework that takes advantage of the suboptimal alignments of the given MSA. Given an input MSA, PSAR-Align first generates suboptimal alignments by probabilistic sampling. Then, for each pair of residues from two different sequences in the input MSA, the number of times they are aligned in the sampled suboptimal alignments is counted and converted to a posterior probability. PSAR-Align uses these probabilities to generate a revised alignment by maximizing the expected accuracy of the MSA. The expected accuracy is defined as the sum of the posterior probabilities of aligned pairs of residues and unaligned single residues in the MSA. In an evaluation based on simulated sequences from five mammalian species, and input alignments from various MSA methods, including MAVID and Pecan, it was shown that the PSAR-Align refinement step generally improved the sensitivity and specificity of the genome alignments.

6.5. Accuracy measures for genome alignment methods

Genome-scale multiple sequence alignments are prerequisites for comparative genomics and evolutionary studies. Therefore, more and more sophisticated analyses rely implicitly on the correctness of these alignments, for example to identify functional genomic elements constrained by purifying selection. Although recent WGA approaches have improved the quality of the automatically constructed alignments, it cannot be assumed that the alignments are correct at all sites across entire genomes. How can we determine which portions of the alignment are reliable and which portions are not, particularly in non-coding regions? In Chapters 4 and 5, we discussed the methods that have classically been used for multiple alignment quality control and aligner benchmarking. However, genome-level alignments present some specificities compared to gene-level alignments, especially for larger or more divergent genomes, where the WGA will contain short conserved regions, separated by large segments that are not homologous and therefore cannot be aligned meaningfully. In this section, we will present the approaches developed more specifically for WGA.

Traditionally, scientists have either assumed that WGAs are generally reliable or they have developed their own filters based on a conservation threshold, for example. Thus, only the regions with high sequence similarity were exploited in the subsequent analyses. This approach is used, for example, in the UCSC whole-genome multiple alignments, which are annotated with PhastCons conservation scores [HUB 11]. PhastCons measures how well-conserved each column of aligned residues is, under the assumption that the alignment is correct, that is those aligned residues are indeed orthologous. The same applies to the scores used in Genomic Evolutionary Rate Profiling (GERP) [COO 05], a statistically rigorous framework for constrained element identification. GERP identifies genomic regions that present nucleotide substitution deficits, and measures these deficits as "rejected substitutions". Rejected substitutions reflect the intensity of past purifying selection and can be used to rank and characterize constrained elements.

Statistical approaches have also been developed to estimate the reliability of WGA. For example, Gumby [PRA 06] is a method that can be used to analyze alignments at any evolutionary distance to identify conserved regions of any size, and, most importantly, to quantify their statistical significance using P-values. Gumby takes its name from the Gumbel distribution, which is the extreme value distribution underlying Karlin–Altschul statistics [KAR 90]. The method requires an alignment, a phylogenetic tree and optional annotations of coding regions as input data. Non-coding regions in the input alignment are used to estimate the neutral mismatch frequency between each pair of aligned sequences. A log-odds scoring scheme for constrained versus neutral evolution is then independently initialized for each pair of sequences. Each alignment column is scored as a sum of pairwise log-odds scores along a circular tour of the phylogenetic tree. Conserved regions appear as stretches of alignment columns with a high aggregate score. The aggregate score of the alignment columns in each conserved region is translated into a P-value using Karlin–Altschul statistics. Gumby is used to annotate the Vista genome browser (www-gsd.lbl.gov/vista/).

Another statistical quality score was introduced specifically for the PSAR-Align realignment program. PSAR score [KIM 11] relies on the suboptimal alignments that are sampled from the posterior probability distribution of an input alignment. Because the direct computation of the posterior probability distribution of MSAs is difficult, it is approximated by pairwise comparisons between each sequence and the rest of the MSA. The pairwise comparison of the preprocessed left-out sequence and subalignment is based on a special type of a pair HMM (pair-HMM) that emits columns of an MSA given the left-out sequence and the subalignment. To obtain the reliability score of an input MSA, the input MSA is then compared with each sampled MSA and the pair scores are averaged over all sampled MSAs.

6.6. Benchmarking genome alignment

The MSA benchmarks described in Chapter 5 mostly contain protein sequence alignments based on 3D structure superpositions. For large non-coding sequences, simulation-based benchmarks have been widely adopted to evaluate alignment accuracy [POL 04, HUA 07, LUN 08]. Nevertheless, the simulation approach is highly dependent on the parameters used to reflect the underlying evolutionary processes and it is not clear whether the resulting simulated sequences mimic real data well enough to compare the biological accuracy of WGA tools. For example, it is known that the conventional simulation approach, which relies on empirically estimated values for various parameters such as substitution rate or insertion/deletion rates, is unable to generate synthetic sequences reflecting the broad genomic variation in conservation levels. A different method for simulating non-coding sequence evolution has been developed [KIM 10], relying on genome-wide distributions of evolutionary parameters rather than their averages. Using this approach, synthetic datasets were generated to mimic orthologous non-coding sequences from the Drosophila group of species, and it was shown that these datasets better represent the variability observed in genomic data in terms of the difficulty of the alignment task. In a comparative study of six WGA tools (including MAVID, MLAGAN and Pecan) using this benchmark, a greater accuracy of multiple alignment tools was observed compared to previous reports. In addition, the authors identified a clear asymmetry in the handling of insertions versus deletions by most alignment tools.

Other methods have been developed to simulate genome sequences, which could potentially be used to evaluate WGA methods. For instance, the EvolSimulator [BEI 07] is a genome simulator, but it has a rather simple model of evolution and is focused on ecological parameters. Another option, the ALF simulator [DAL 12], models gene and neutral DNA evolution. The EVOLVER software (www.drive5.com/evolver) can simulate full-sized, multichromosome genome evolution in forward time. EVOLVER models DNA sequence evolution with sequence annotations, a gene model, an evolutionary constraint model, chromosomal rearrangements, tandem and segmental duplications as well as mobile element insertions, movements and evolution.

Recently, a competition was organized, called Alignathon [EAR 14], to assess WGA methods. Two datasets were simulated using the EVOLVER tool, starting from primate and mammalian phylogenies, and one dataset was composed of 20 real fly genomes. In total, 12 different alignment methods were assessed. Using the simulated datasets where the true alignment was known, many of the submissions were able to align the primate dataset with relatively high recall and precision. For the mammalian simulations, the results were more dissimilar, with Cactus performing better than the other methods tested. Concerning the different annotation types, submissions were generally best in genic regions, where simulated selection led to strong conservation. Performance was intermediate in neutral regions and submissions generally performed most poorly in repetitive regions. When using the real fly genomes, where the true alignment is not known, statistical assessment with PSAR-Align was used to estimate the quality of the alignments constructed by the different methods. The results of the statistical assessments generally agreed with the simulation-based experiments, and indicated that there are substantial accuracy differences between the alignment tools tested.

WGA benchmarking is an ongoing process and a number of questions remain to be answered. For example, no systematic studies have been dedicated to comparing the quality of WGA tools with methods for other types of MSA, such as protein aligners, or how the quality of the input genomes and their assemblies affects WGAs. Nevertheless, efforts such as Alignathon should help pave the way for subsequent benchmarking efforts with more datasets and accurate statistical assessments, and will hopefully contribute to the improvement of WGA tools in the future.

7

Multiple Alignment of Thousands of Sequences

The genome sequencing of numerous organisms has hugely increased the number of sequences available in both the nucleotide and protein databases. For example, Figure 7.1 shows the exponential growth of the UniProtKB (www.ebi.ac.uk/uniprot) protein database, an annotated collection of publicly available protein sequences since 1997. Specialist protein resources, such as the Pfam, UniprotKB or RefSeq databases, are classifying these sequences into families that can contain >100,000 members and these families will continue to expand as new genomes are sequenced [HOL 15]. As a result, multiple alignments of many thousands of protein sequences have becoming a commonplace application.

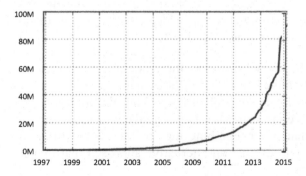

Figure 7.1. *Exponential growth of entries in the UniProtKB protein sequence database*

These raw data clearly provide new opportunities for large-scale genome-level or systems-level studies, although there is a question about the exploitability of such very large alignments. On the one hand, some authors [SIM 05, PEI 07] have suggested that adding more sequences can increase the quality of a multiple alignment. On the other hand, this is only true if the new sequences are carefully chosen. Recent studies [THO 11, SIE 13] have demonstrated that in fact alignment quality decreases for larger numbers of sequences when these sequences included fragments or errors.

One of the main reasons for this is the nature of the new sequence data. First, the generation of a very large scale MSA using the traditional alignment methods can be computationally too intensive. Shortcuts have therefore been introduced that reduce the time and memory complexity, but also reduce alignment quality. Second, high-throughput biological datasets are notoriously incomplete, noisy and inconsistent and DNA or protein sequences are no exception [PRO 12]. A number of recent studies have investigated the rate of errors in NGS genome data and their impact on the accuracy of downstream analyses   [EL 13]. For protein studies, the DNA sequencing errors are further confounded by inaccuracies in the delineation of the protein-coding genes, since coding regions are mostly predicted by automatic methods that are not completely accurate [DEN 14]. Analyses have shown that, for the genes that are identified in genome sequences, the complete exon/intron structure is correctly predicted for only about 50–60% of them [HAR 09]. In eukaryotic genomes, the situation is also complicated by widespread alternative splicing events, which affects more than 92–94% of multiexon human genes [HAL 10].

This chapter will discuss the strategies developed to address the challenges linked to aligning large datasets containing thousands of sequences. First, we will describe how the traditional aligners have evolved to cope with very large numbers of sequences and the meta-aligners that try to combine the advantages of different algorithms. Then, we will discuss an alternative approach that involves gradually adding new sequences to a high-quality seed alignment. Finally, the benchmark sets constructed to evaluate the new large-scale alignment tools will be presented.

7.1. Extension of the progressive alignment approach

Most traditional aligners are based on the "progressive alignment" heuristic, which aligns sequences in larger subalignments, following the branching order specified by a guide tree. With a complexity of roughly $O(n^2)$ for n sequences, this approach can routinely make alignments of hundreds of sequences of moderate length, but large servers are generally required to make alignments much bigger than this. Nevertheless, a few of the standard aligners can be used to align more than a thousand sequences. For example, Kalign version 2 [LAS 09] is a progressive aligner like its predecessor, but the original Wu–Manber algorithm has been replaced with the faster Muth– Manber string matching algorithm for the construction of pairwise alignments, and the space-saving Myers and Miller algorithm [MYE 88] is used during the multiple alignment step. The MAFFT suite [KAT 02] has also undergone a number of improvements over the years since its initial introduction, many of them dedicated to improving the running time and accuracy of large-scale alignments. One of the limiting steps of the MAFFT progressive alignment, in terms of computational time, was the construction of the guide tree. Therefore, the authors developed the PartTree algorithm [KAT 07], which yields guide tree construction times of complexity $O(n \log n)$. The new version of MAFFT with the PartTree algorithm can align up to 60,000 sequences in several minutes on a standard desktop computer. The loss of accuracy in MSA caused by this tree approximation was estimated to be several percent in benchmark tests using data from the Pfam database. In a recent comparison study of different tree construction methods [YAM 16], a simple chained guide tree approach [BOY 14] with complexity $O(n)$ was used to add individual sequences to a growing alignment in an arbitrary order. Although this is a very fast method, the resulting alignments were clearly less accurate for some tests.

Clustal Omega [SIE 11] is a new progressive aligner that is a completely revised version of the widely used Clustal series of programs. It can handle tens of thousands of DNA/RNA or protein sequences. Clustal Omega uses a modified version of the mBed algorithm [BLA 10], which has complexity of $O(n \log n)$ (like PartTree), and which produces guide trees that are as accurate as those from conventional methods. mBed works by "embedding" each sequence in a space of t dimensions where $t = (\log2 \ n)^2$. Each sequence is then replaced by a t element vector, representing the distances between the sequence and t "seed sequences". These vectors can be clustered extremely quickly by standard methods, such as K-means or UPGMA, in order to build rough guide trees. The multiple alignments are then built using the accurate HHalign package [SÖD 05], which aligns two profile HMMs.

7.2. Meta-aligners for large numbers of sequences

SATé [LIU 09] is a meta-method that can construct large alignments and phylogenetic trees simultaneously in practical time frames. It does this by building an initial alignment/tree using an existing MSA method, and then performs hill-climbing searches to find an optimal alignment/tree with an ML score. For its starting alignment/tree pair, SATé selects among four tree/alignment pairs by running RAxML on four alignments (ClustalW, Muscle, MAFFT and Prank) and picks the pair with the best ML score on its tree. In each iteration, a new alignment is proposed by a divide-and-conquer method, called center-tree-i decomposition, which divides the complete tree into smaller subtrees. Sequences in each subtree are realigned using MAFFT, and the subalignments are progressively merged using Muscle. The speed and accuracy of SATé were improved in a new version, SATé-II [LIU 12], which uses a different divide-and-conquer strategy guaranteed to produce small subtrees with more similar sequences. In addition, the Muscle aligner was replaced by OPAL [WHE 07] for merging subalignments. Finally, SATé-II uses only MAFFT as its starting point, rather than computing four different initial alignments. SATé-II was shown to improve alignment quality compared to the initial methods, and the trees based upon these improved alignments were also more accurate.

SATé-II and OPAL were also used in a more recent method, called Practical Alignments using SATé and TrAnsitivity (PASTA) [MIR 15]. PASTA works by iteratively dividing an alignment into overlapping subproblems. At each iteration, subproblems are each aligned independently using the accurate MAFFT consistency-based approach. Then, pairs of MSAs are aligned together using OPAL. The resulting collection of compatible MSAs overlap with each other and can be merged using transitivity to generate an MSA on the entire set of sequences. In a study using biological and simulated data with up to 200,000 sequences, it was shown that PASTA improved the accuracy and scalability of the leading alignment methods (including SATé).

Finally, the PASTA method was incorporated into UPP for "Ultra-large alignments using Phylogeny-aware Profiles" [NGU 15]. UPP is an MSA method specifically designed to take into account the many fragmentary sequences that are now present in protein sequence databases. The algorithm has four steps. Step 1 selects a subset of the input sequences called the "backbone dataset" that specifically excludes the fragmentary sequences: the remaining sequences are the "query sequences". Step 2 uses PASTA to compute an MSA and ML tree on the backbone sequences. Step 3 creates an ensemble of HMMs from the backbone alignment and backbone tree. Step 4 inserts the remaining query sequences, including fragments, into the backbone alignments and transitivity is used to merge all sequences into a final alignment. This means that UPP is highly robust to fragmentary data and in most cases it produces alignments with higher quality than PASTA.

7.3. Extending "seed" alignments

The *ab initio* construction of a full multiple alignment is not the only way to make very large alignments. A more efficient approach is to take a high-quality, often expert curated, MSA and incorporate new sequences as they become available. The resulting alignment also retains biological knowledge that was incorporated into the expert alignment. This approach has been used for some time to construct the very large multiple alignments in the Pfam database [FIN 15]. For each Pfam entry corresponding to a known protein domain, a representative subset of the entire set of matching sequences are first aligned to make a "seed" alignment. As this alignment generally contains a small number of sequences, highly accurate methods and manual curation can be used. The seed alignment is then used to construct a profile HMM and all other members of the domain family are aligned to the profile HMM to generate the "full" alignment. Unfortunately, the accuracy of the full alignments constructed using this strategy is generally lower than the smaller seed alignments.

Similar options to use a preexisting HMM to help the alignment of a new set of sequences are also provided in the Clustal Omega aligner [SIE 11]. The MAFFT package also contains options to add unaligned sequences into an existing alignment [KAT 12]. A standard global alignment method is provided for adding full-length sequences, while for handling short unaligned sequences a rapid local alignment method is used.

In addition to protein sequence alignments, the needs for aligning short DNA sequences have increased recently with the application of NGS methods for *in vivo* sampling of microbial communities (e.g. in the environment, in the human gut or on the skin). The first step in studies of such meta-genomic data is to identify the biological origin of the reads by assigning the reads to a reference phylogeny. The reference phylogeny is a fully resolved phylogenetic tree that is based on a reference multiple alignment of the full-length sequences in the tree. While the Clustal Omega and MAFFT options described above can be used for this task, other algorithms have been developed with more sophisticated phylogenetic models. For example, PaPaRa [BER 11] is a parsimony-based, phylogeny-aware, short read alignment tool. The underlying idea of PaPaRa is to align the short read sequences against the ancestral state vector of each edge in the reference tree. These ancestral state sequences are conceptually similar to profile HMMs, but do not use a probabilistic model because of prohibitive run times. The alignment of the reads against each ancestral state vector is carried out by a standard dynamic programming algorithm for pairwise alignment. Pagan [LÖY 12] is another method for phylogeny-aware alignment based on partial-order sequence graphs. It is based on the same principle as PRANK (see section 4.2) and uses evolutionary information to distinguish insertions from deletions. In order to extend existing alignments, PAGAN first infers ancestral sequences for the reference alignment and then adds new sequences in their phylogenetic context, either to predefined positions or by finding the best placement for sequences of unknown origin. The key advantage of the graph representation is the ability to represent uncertainties in the unaligned sequences or in the inferred ancestral sequences.

7.4. Benchmarking large numbers of sequences

In order to evaluate and compare the performances of the different large-scale aligners, benchmark tests are needed that contain alignments with thousands of sequences. One obvious solution is to use simulated sequences (discussed in Chapter 5), since this approach can obviously allow for arbitrary numbers of sequences in the test alignments. Unfortunately, simulated sequences are inherently dependent on the simplified models of evolution used and may not realistically model real proteins.

Some of the earliest large-scale benchmark datasets using real sequences were based on ribosomal RNA sequence alignments, such as those on the Comparative RNA Website (CRW) (www.rna.ccbb.utexas.edu). For example, the bacterial 16S rRNA alignment contains >35,000 sequences. The curated alignments provided in CRW are based upon secondary structural information. Since then, more diverse benchmarks have been constructed by combining the smaller benchmarks, such as HOMSTRAD or BaliBASE, with the large number of sequences available in the Pfam database. An example of such a large-scale benchmark is the HomFam data set [BLA 10], which uses structural alignments from HOMSTRAD combined with Pfam entries containing up to 10,000 sequences. The benchmark thus allows the evaluation of computational times for increasing numbers of sequences. However, the quality of the complete MSA is not estimated. The alignment score depends only on the alignment of the small fraction of HOMSTRAD sequences and misalignments of Pfam sequences are not taken into account. A similar benchmark, called BaliFam [SIE 13], combined reference sequences from BAliBASE with ≥1,000 Pfam sequences. The advantage of BAliBASE is that it contains multidomain families in contrast to HOMSTRAD. The ability of a wide range of widely used MSA packages to align large sequence sets were evaluated using these benchmarks, and it was shown that the accuracy of the alignments decreases markedly as the number of sequences grows. The strategy that best preserves alignment accuracy with very large datasets is to use a very high quality seed alignment of a small subset of the sequences to help guide the alignment. This suggests that very large alignments of high quality may be possible, but only if very high quality alignments such as those from structure superpositions or expert curated alignments are available.

Although these structure-based benchmarks may contain alignments with many sequences, the aligners are only evaluated based on the reference alignment of a small subset of sequences contained in the MSA. This could allow large errors in non-reference sequences to go undetected. In addition, the structure-based reference alignment must itself be created, and this alignment depends on heuristic structure comparison algorithms. An alternative approach was used to construct the ContTest benchmark [FOX 15]. ContTest predicts a contact map for a selected protein with a known 3D structure in the MSA to be tested. All the sequences in the alignment are taken into account to predict this contact map. The predicted contact map is then compared with the known contact map for the same protein, and the alignment is scored based on their agreement. This process gives a very robust scoring system based on the assumption that better alignments will result in more accurate contact maps. ContTest contains 136 test cases with between 1,467 and 43,910 sequences.

The benchmark was used to score alignments made by diverse aligners. The ContTest benchmark was in general agreement with structure-based benchmarks (like HomFam) for large numbers of sequences, with Kalign and HMMT obtaining the best scores. Nevertheless, the ranking of some methods differed between ContTest and HomFam, notably for Clustal Omega that obtained high HomFam scores but low ContTest scores. Another limitation of this benchmark is that all alignments involve only sequences of a single protein domain, without any large insertions. It is likely that certain methods might perform poorly on more general alignment problems involving multiple domains and non-collinear regions. Further benchmarks are still needed to address such highly complex test cases.

8

Future Perspectives: High-Performance Computing

In parallel with the development of genome sequencing technologies, the context in computer science is also changing rapidly. Throughout the 1980s and 1990s, CPUs were able to run virtually any kind of software twice as fast every 18–20 months, in accordance with Moore's law (Figure 8.1). But eventually, at some point around 2005, a plateau was reached with 3.6 GHz for Intel CPUs. Beyond this, complex cooling systems are required that cannot be easily implemented in standard workstations or clusters. Moore's law is still valid, although the performance gains are now accomplished in fundamentally different ways. Transistor density on silicon continues to double every 2 years because of multithread and multicore features.

As a result, the future of sequential algorithms is not bright; as by essence, they can only run on one core, and the clock frequency of single cores is slowing down. The only way to follow future developments in hardware is to develop parallel algorithms that can take advantage of a large number of processing cores. But this is easier said than done, because not all problems are inherently parallelizable and because parallel programming is hard.

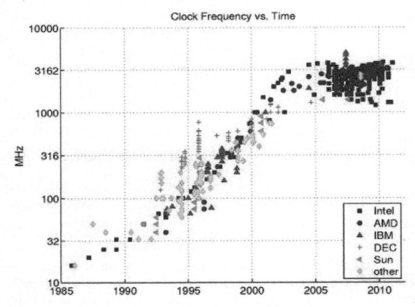

Figure 8.1. *Evolution of CPU clock speed. Data from the Stanford CPU database (cpudb.stanford.edu). For a color version of the figure, see www.iste.co.uk/thompson/statistics.zip*

In the field of multiple sequence alignment, a number of groups have turned to the new computational architectures to cope with the huge amounts of sequence data now available in the public databases. This chapter will discuss three promising solutions for future developments. First, coarse grain parallelism can be achieved on multicore CPUs where each core is a complete independent CPU or on a computational grid, where a number of distributed computers run independent tasks and are linked by the Internet or other networks. Second, fine-grain parallelism can be attained on general purpose graphics processing units (GPU) that implement simplified cores, allowing them to fit many more cores on a single chip. Finally, cloud computing can provide users with on-demand access to shared computing resources (e.g. servers, storage, applications and services) over the Internet.

8.1. Coarse-grain parallelism: grid computing

In the context of high-performance computing (HPC), the traditional solutions for distributed architectures are represented by computer clusters and grid computing. Although these infrastructures are characterized by some considerable drawbacks, in general they are largely used by the scientific community because they can be used to execute the available computational methods with minimal changes to the existing CPU code with the exception of possible modifications necessary for message passing.

There are parallel implementations for many of the main progressive alignment methods (described in Chapter 2), which all share two major steps: pairwise alignments for the guide tree construction and the progressive multiple alignment step. There is no problem in the parallelization of the first stage of pairwise alignments, since these can be processed simultaneously and independently. In the progressive alignment stage, larger and larger groups of sequences are aligned. This process is difficult to parallelize, because the order of the alignment calculations is fixed by the guide tree: an alignment at a node cannot be performed until all of the alignments in its child nodes have been completed. If this restriction is maintained, alignments can be performed at child nodes that are independent of each other. Nevertheless, the efficiency of parallelization is generally low in this stage.

SGI's commercial parallel version of Clustal was the first attempt to accelerate ClustalW by parallelizing all three stages, although it ran only on a shared memory SGI Origin machine using OpenMP. It showed a speedup of up to 10-fold when running on 16 CPUs. ClustalW-MPI [LI 03] was targeted for more general workstation clusters with a distributed memory architecture. It also parallelized all three stages of the progressive alignment and achieved an overall speedup of 4.3 using 16 CPUs. Because ClustalW-MPI uses a RAM memory-storage mode, it has the inherent problem of a shortage of memory when trying to align larger data sets. ClustalXeed [KIM 10] was designed to simultaneously address the dual needs of fast computation by providing enhanced job scheduling and large sequence data handling by supporting disk-memory access capabilities. Tests showed an average speed-up of about 19.6 using 50 nodes on a 100 CPU cluster system.

Parallel T-Coffee [ZOL 07] was the first parallel implementation of T-Coffee, which combines a consistency-based scoring function with the progressive alignment algorithm. The T-Coffee algorithm works in two main stages. In the first stage, a list of pairwise alignments is constructed and stored in a library. Then, during the second progressive alignment stage, the library is used to evaluate the subalignments. Both these stages have been parallelized, based on message passing and remote memory access mechanisms. Parallel T-Coffee realized a speedup of about 3 with 80 processors on a cluster consisting of dual Intel Xeon 3GHz nodes. Most of the speedup comes from parallelizing and distributing pairwise alignment tasks with dynamic scheduling for a near linear speedup during library generations.

The MAFFT aligner has also been parallelized in Parallel-MAFFT [KAT 10], using the POSIX Threads library. It targets a specific type of PC, which has one or two processors, each with up to four cores, and shared memory space. In addition to the initial progressive alignment, MAFFT includes a final iterative refinement, where an alignment is divided into two subalignments, and then the two subalignments are realigned to obtain an alignment with a higher objective score. This stage was parallelized using a simple hill-climbing approach. Realignment processes are randomly assigned to multiple threads and performed in parallel. If the score of a new alignment by a thread is better than the original alignment, then it replaces the original alignment. This approach was tested on a 16 core PC and achieved a speedup of 10.

Parallel versions of some of the statistical alignment approaches (described in Chapter 4) are also available. For example, MSAProbs [LIU 10] works by (i) calculating all pairwise posterior probability matrices using a pair-HMM and a partition function; (ii) constructing a guide tree from the posterior probability matrices and (iii) performing a weighted probabilistic consistency transformation of all pairwise posterior probability matrices and computing a progressive alignment using these matrices. By default, the algorithm is optimized for multicore CPUs by employing OpenMP (www.openmp.org), an application programming interface (API) for multithreaded, shared-memory parallel programming. MSACompro [DEN 11] follows the general scheme implemented in MSAProbs, but it incorporates secondary structure and solvent accessibility information in the calculation of the posterior residue–residue alignment probabilities and computes the pairwise distance matrix with the help of predicted residue–residue contact information. MSACompro is slower than MSAProbs since it needs to generate extra structural information for the alignment. In tests on the BAliBASE benchmark, when one CPU core was used, it took MSACompro around 6 days and 14 h to predict secondary structure and solvent accessibility information. This time was reduced to < 5 ho by using a multiple-threading implementation on a 32 core machine.

8.2. Fine-grain parallelism: GPGPU

GPUs are gaining popularity, as they are pervasive, relatively cheap and extremely efficient parallel multicore coprocessors, giving access to low-cost, energy-efficient means to achieve tera-scale performances on common workstations, or even peta-scale performances on GPU-equipped supercomputers [NOB 16]. GPUs, which typically handled computation only for computer graphics, have also been exploited to perform more general purpose computations (GPGPUs), including applications traditionally handled by the CPU. Early efforts to use GPUs as general-purpose processors around 2001 required reformulating computational problems in terms of graphics primitives. Later, Nvidia's compute unified device architecture (CUDA), Microsoft's DirectCompute and Apple/Khronos Group's OpenCL allowed programmers to ignore the underlying graphical concepts in favor of more common HPC concepts. This means that modern GPGPU pipelines can leverage the speed of a GPU without requiring full and explicit conversion of the data to a graphical form.

Even though a single GPU core is four times slower than a CPU core, GPUs are much more powerful than CPUs because of their massive parallelism. The main drawback is the simplified architecture of GPU chips, which imposes many programming constraints. Typically, GPUs are Single Program Multiple Data parallel processors, meaning that all processors must execute the same instruction at the same time. There are therefore two ways to program GPUs.

The first option involves porting an existing sequential algorithm onto the cards, but the specificities of GPUs are such that it is difficult to exploit them in an optimal way. For instance, ClustalW has been adapted for GPU systems in MSA-CUDA [LIU 09], which parallelizes all three stages of the ClustalW processing pipeline for the GPU using CUDA. It demonstrates average speedups between 11 and 36 on a GeForce GTX 280 GPU against a Pentium IV. MAFFT has also been optimized for GPUs [ZHU 15] and tested in three NVIDIA GPUs achieving a speedup up to 11.28 on a Tesla K20m GPU compared to the sequential MAFFT. QuickProbs [GUD 14] is a variant of MSAProbs where the two most time-consuming stages of MSAProbs are redesigned for GPU execution: the posterior matrices calculation and the consistency transformation. Experiments on three popular benchmarks (BAliBASE, PREFAB and OXBench) on a quad-core PC equipped with a high-end graphics card showed that QuickProbs is 5.7–9.7 times faster than the original CPU-parallel MSAProbs. Additional tests performed on several protein families from the Pfam database gave an overall speedup of 6.7.

The second option is to accept the architecture of the GPU cards and use an algorithm that matches it as closely as possible, allowing for a much better speedup. Evolutionary algorithms, especially genetic algorithms, are good candidates to be ported onto such an architecture, since the same genetic operators such as crossover and mutation can be applied simultaneously to different members of the population

[MAI 12]. For a generic local search algorithm based on an evolutionary algorithm, the typical speedup using a GeForce GTX 280 GPU versus an Intel Core i7 950 is around 100×. The parallel hybrid genetic algorithm [NGU 03] uses a progressive alignment algorithm to create the initial subpopulations and a genetic algorithm to refine them. A coarse-grained parallelization, where subpopulation evolution occurs on separate processors with periodic migration, achieved a speed up of 6.6 on an eight processor cluster in tests using the BALiBASE benchmark. Non-dominating sorting genetic algorithm (NSGA-II) [D'AG 15] is a multiobjective evolutionary algorithm, representing a general technique that is useful for solving many multiobjective optimization tasks in computational biology, such as feature classification, gene clustering, sequence alignment or protein structure prediction. A full parallelization of the NSGA-II algorithm is available for the CUDA platform. Simulations on benchmark multiobjective optimization problems showed that the parallelization presented speedups of the order of 130 compared with a sequential implementation of the non-dominated sorting procedure.

Another type of nature-inspired algorithm, known as swarm intelligence, includes mainly stochastic search and optimization techniques, guided by the principles of collective behavior and self-organization of insect swarms. They are efficient, adaptive and robust search methods producing near optimal solutions. Like genetic algorithms, swarm intelligence algorithms have a large amount of implicit parallelism. An example of a swarm intelligence algorithm is particle swarm optimization (PSO), inspired by social behavior of bird flocking or fish schooling. PSO is initialized with a population of random solutions and searches for optima by updating generations. The potential solutions, called particles, fly through the problem space by following the current optimum particles. GPU-SPSO [ZHO 09] is a parallel GPU version of PSO based on the CUDA. GPU-SPSO allowed larger swarm populations and greatly improved running time compared to the sequential version, and thus provided users with a feasible solution for a wide variety of complex optimization problems. PSO has been used to construct global MSA [KAM 12]. In this system, each particle represents a possible alignment and contains all the sequences. An initial alignment is constructed using any MSA method and used to generate other particles by making random insertions. In the parallel version, the particles are divided over the available processors. At the end of each iteration, all processors communicate to determine the new leader and exchange sequences. Experimental results using different tests from the SABmark and BAliBASE benchmark databases showed that the algorithm could be used effectively to increase the accuracy of the initial input alignment.

8.3. MSA in the cloud

Another possible solution to the infrastructure challenge comes in the form of "cloud computing", a model where computation and storage exist as virtual resources, accessed via the Internet, which can be dynamically allocated and released as needed. Where previously acquisition of large amounts of computing power required significant initial and ongoing costs, the cloud model radically alters this by allowing computing resources and services to be acquired and paid for on demand. Importantly, cloud resources can provide storage and computation at far less cost than dedicated resources for certain use cases. Cloud resources have become quite popular in the form of public clouds (e.g. Amazon Web Services [AWS], HP Cloud, Google Compute Engine) where we pay only for the resources consumed. Over the past few years, there has been an increasing trend toward cloud resources also becoming available as research infrastructures, for example the Open Science Data Cloud (www.opensciencedatacloud.org) or the EGI Federated Cloud (www.egi.eu/infrastructure/cloud).

For multiple sequence alignment construction, the effective use of cloud resources has been demonstrated by the porting of the T-Coffee tool onto the cloud [DI 10]. In general, utilization of bioinformatics tools on such delocalized systems requires technical expertise to achieve robust operation and intended performance gains. In trying to address this, significant work has been undertaken to develop workflow environments that attempt to alleviate the need for scientists to write their own scripts or programs. There are several engines that give users the ability to design and execute workflows, including multiple sequence alignment among many other applications. Each engine was created to address certain problems of a specific community, therefore each one has its advantages and shortcomings. Some of the environments that integrate aligners in the Cloud include the following:

– Galaxy Cloud [AFG 11] allows a user to run a private installation of the Galaxy framework in the cloud. Galaxy (galaxyproject.org) is a popular open-source platform designed to make complex analyses available to researchers using nothing more than a web browser. It allows the construction of complex workflows, and allows the results to be documented, shared and published, guaranteeing transparency and reproducibility. An active community of developers ensures that the latest tools (mainly for NGS data analysis) are wrapped and made available through the Galaxy Tool Shed. Galaxy Cloud exactly replicates the functionality of the main Galaxy site in the cloud. Currently, Galaxy Cloud is deployed on the AWS cloud, although it should be compatible with other clouds. Galaxy Cloud's deployment is achieved by coupling the Galaxy framework to CloudMan [AFG 12], which automates management of the underlying infrastructure cloud resources, including resource acquisition, configuration and data persistence.

– BioNode [PRI 12] allows a bioinformatics workflow to be modeled and executed in virtual machines (VMs) in different cloud environments. BioNode is based on Debian Linux and can be deployed on several operating systems (Windows, OSX, Linux), architectures as well as in the cloud. Approximately 200 bioinformatics programs mostly related to evolutionary analyses are included. Examples of representative software implemented in BioNode are Muscle and MAFFT for multiple sequence alignment or PAML and MrBayes for phylogenetic tree construction. In addition, BioNode configuration allows scripts to parallelize these bioinformatics tools.

– Cloud BioLinux [KRA 12] is a publicly accessible VM that enables scientists to quickly provision on-demand infrastructures for high-performance bioinformatics computing using cloud platforms. Users have access to a range of preconfigured command line and graphical software applications, including over >100 bioinformatics packages for applications including sequence alignment, clustering, assembly, display, editing and phylogeny. The VM is deployed on the Amazon EC2 cloud, but it is also compatible with other clouds.

– Tavaxy [ABO 13] is a system for modeling and executing bioinformatics workflows based on the integration of the Taverna (www.taverna.org.uk) and Galaxy (galaxyproject.org) workflow environments. Tavaxy supports execution in a sequential environment or on HPC infrastructures and cloud computing systems. It offers a set of features that simplify the development of sequence analysis applications, covering several areas of bioinformatics such as NGS data analysis, metagenomics, proteomics or comparative genomics. Tavaxy can be downloaded or directly used as a service in clouds.

– Yabi [HUN 12] provides a workflow environment that can create and reuse workflows as well as manage large amounts of raw and processed data in a secure and flexible way across geographically distributed HPC resources. It includes a frontend web application that provides the main user interface; middleware that is responsible for process management, tool configuration, analysis audit trails and user management; and a resource manager that provides data and compute services, including a list of bioinformatics tools running in various execution environments. In this way, Yabi gives researchers access to HPC power without requiring specialized computing knowledge.

The use of cloud computing for biological sequence analysis is only going to increase, but as the datasets grow in size, the resources underpinning the analysis environment must be low cost, scalable and easily accessible for the whole community. Ideally, minimal preparations and resources should be necessary before obtaining access to an analysis environment that is genuinely useful. Nevertheless, to provide flexibility and performance, the user must have some control of the data resources and software tools via a lightweight programming or graphical interface. High-speed transfer technologies are also critical for moving large amounts of data in and out of the cloud. Although larger organizations with enough computational expertise may prefer to develop and maintain their own in-house systems, cloud computing will save resources for smaller groups, allowing them to concentrate on the main task, namely the biological interpretation of the analysis results.

Bibliography

[ABO 13] ABOUELHODA M., ISSA, S., "Towards scalable and cost-aware bioinformatics workflow execution in the cloud – recent advances to the tavaxy workflow system", *Fundamenta Informaticae*, vol. 128, no. 3, pp. 255–280, 2013.

[AFG 11] AFGAN E., BAKER D., CORAOR N. *et al.*, "Harnessing cloud computing with Galaxy Cloud", *Nature Biotechnology*, vol. 29, no. 11, pp. 972–974, 2011.

[AFG 12] AFGAN E., CHAPMAN B., TAYLOR J., "CloudMan as a platform for tool, data, and analysis distribution", *BMC Bioinformatics*, vol. 13, no. 1, p. 315, 2012.

[AGG 02] AGGARWAL G., RAMASWAMY R., "*Ab initio* gene identification: prokaryote genome annotation with GeneScan and GLIMMER", *Journal of Bioscience*, vol. 27, no. suppl 1, pp. 7–14, 2002.

[AHL 06] AHLQUIST P., "Parallels among positive-strand RNA viruses, reverse-transcribing viruses and double-stranded RNA viruses", *Nature Reviews*, Microbiology, vol. 4, no. 5, pp. 371–382, 2006.

[ALT 96] ALTSCHUL S.F., GISH W., "Local alignment statistics", *Methods Enzymology*, vol. 266, pp. 460–480, 1996.

[ALT 97] ALTSCHUL S.F., MADDEN T.L., SCHAFFER A.A. *et al.*, "Gapped BLAST and PSI-BLAST: a new generation of protein database search programs", *Nucleic Acids Research*, vol. 25, no. 17, pp. 3389–3402, 1997.

[ANG 11] ANGIUOLI S.V., SALZBERG S.L., "Mugsy: fast multiple alignment of closely related whole genomes", *Bioinformatics*, vol. 27, no. 3, pp. 334–342, 2011.

[ANI 10] ANIBA M.R., POCH O., THOMPSON J.D., "Issues in bioinformatics benchmarking: the case study of multiple sequence alignment", *Nucleic Acids Research*, vol. 38, no. 21, pp. 7353–7363, 2010.

[BAR 87] BARTON G.J., STERNBERG M.J., "A strategy for the rapid multiple alignment of protein sequences. Confidence levels from tertiary structure comparisons", *Journal of Molecular Biology*, vol. 198, no. 2, pp. 327–337, 1987.

[BAR 16] BARSON G., GRIFFITHS E., "SeqTools: visual tools for manual analysis of sequence alignments", *BMC Research Notes*, vol. 9, p. 39, 2016.

[BAW 14] BAWONO P., HERINGA J., "PRALINE: a versatile multiple sequence alignment toolkit", *Methods in Molecular Biology*, vol. 1079, pp. 245–262, 2014.

[BAW 15] BAWONO P., VAN DER VELDE A., ABELN S. *et al.*, "Quantifying the displacement of mismatches in multiple sequence alignment benchmarks", *PLoS ONE*, vol. 10, no. 5, p. e0127431, 2015.

[BEI 07] BEIKO R.G., CHARLEBOIS R.L., "A simulation test bed for hypotheses of genome evolution", *Bioinformatics*, vol. 23, no. 7, pp. 825–831, 2007.

[BEN 93] BENNER S.A., COHEN M.A., GONNET G.H., "Empirical and structural models for insertions and deletions in the divergent evolution of proteins", *Journal of Molecular Biology*, vol. 229, no. 4, pp. 1065–1082, 1993.

[BER 11] BERGER S.A., STAMATAKIS A., "Aligning short reads to reference alignments and trees", *Bioinformatics*, vol. 27, no. 15, pp. 2068–2075, 2011.

[BER 14] BERMEJO-DAS-NEVES C., NGUYEN H.N., POCH O. *et al.*, "A comprehensive study of small non-frameshift insertions/deletions in proteins and prediction of their phenotypic effects by a machine learning method (KD4i)", *BMC Bioinformatics*, vol. 15, no. 1, p. 111, 2014.

[BIS 86] BISHOP M.J., THOMPSON E.A., "Maximum likelihood alignment of DNA sequences", *Journal of Molecular Biology*, vol. 190, no. 2, pp. 159–165, 1986.

[BLA 04] BLANCHETTE M., KENT W.J., RIEMER C. *et al.*, "Aligning multiple genomic sequences with the threaded blockset aligner", *Genome Research*, vol. 14, no. 4, pp. 708–715, 2004.

[BLA 10] BLACKSHIELDS G., SIEVERS F., SHI W. *et al.*, "Sequence embedding for fast construction of guide trees for multiple sequence alignment", *Algorithms for Molecular Biology*, vol. 5, p. 21, 2010.

[BLA 13] BLACKBURNE B.P., WHELAN S., "Class of multiple sequence alignment algorithm affects genomic analysis", *Molecular Biology and Evolution*, vol. 30, no. 3, pp. 642–653, 2013.

[BON 01] BONNEAU R., STRAUSS C.E., BAKER D., "Improving the performance of Rosetta using multiple sequence alignment information and global measures of hydrophobic core formation", *Proteins*, vol. 43, no. 1, pp. 1–11, 2001.

[BOY 14] BOYCE K., SIEVERS F., HIGGINS D.G., "Simple chained guide trees give high-quality protein multiple sequence alignments", *Proceedings of the National Academy of Sciences*, vol. 111, no. 29, pp. 10556–10561, 2014.

[BRA 03a] BRAY N., DUBCHAK I., PACHTER L., "AVID: a global alignment program", *Genome Research*, vol. 13, no. 1, pp. 97–102, 2003.

[BRA 03b] BRAY N., PACHTER L., "MAVID multiple alignment server", *Nucleic Acids Research*, vol. 31, no. 13, pp. 3525–3526, 2003.

[BRA 09] BRADLEY R.K., ROBERT A., SMOOT M. *et al.*, "Fast statistical alignment", *PLoS Computational Biology*, vol. 5, no. 5, p. e1000392, 2009.

[BRO 09] BROOKS B.R., BROOKS C.L., MACKERELL A.D. *et al.*, "CHARMM: the biomolecular simulation program", *Journal of Computational Chemistry*, vol. 30, no. 10, pp. 1545–1614, 2009.

[BRU 03] BRUDNO M., DO C.B., COOPER G.M. *et al.*, "LAGAN and Multi-LAGAN: efficient tools for large-scale multiple alignment of genomic DNA", *Genome Research*, vol. 13, no. 4, pp. 721–731, 2003.

[BUR 14] BURKI F., "The eukaryotic tree of life from a global phylogenomic perspective", *Cold Spring Harbor Perspectives in Biology*, vol. 6, no. 5, p. a016147, 2014.

[CAI 00] CAI L., JUEDES D., LIAKHOVITCH E., "Evolutionary computation techniques for multiple sequence alignment", *Proceedings of the 2000 Congress on Evolutionary Computation CEC00 Cat No00TH8512*, vol. 2, pp. 829–835, 2000.

[CAR 88] CARRILLO H., LIPMAN D., "The multiple sequence alignment problem in biology", *SIAM Journal on Applied Mathematics*, vol. 48, pp. 1073–1082, 1988.

[CEC 14] CECH T.R., STEITZ J.A., "The noncoding RNA revolution – trashing old rules to forge new ones", *Cell*, vol. 157, no. 1, pp. 77–94, 2014.

[CHA 06] CHAKRABARTI S., LANCZYCKI C.J., PANCHENKO A.R. *et al.*, "Refining multiple sequence alignments with conserved core regions", *Nucleic Acids Research*, vol. 34, no. 9, pp. 2598–2606, 2006.

[CHA 12] CHANG J.M., DI TOMMASO P., TALY J.F. *et al.*, "Accurate multiple sequence alignment of transmembrane proteins with PSI-Coffee", *BMC Bioinformatics*, vol. 13, no. suppl 4, p. S1, 2012.

[CHA 14] CHANG J.M., DI TOMMASO P., NOTREDAME C., "TCS: a new multiple sequence alignment reliability measure to estimate alignment accuracy and improve phylogenetic tree reconstruction", *Molecular Biology and Evolution*, vol. 31, no. 6, pp. 1625–1637, 2014.

[CHE 99] CHELLAPILLA K., FOGEL G.B., "Multiple sequence alignment using evolutionary programming", *Proceedings of the 1999 Congress on Evolutionary Computation CEC99 Cat No 99TH8406*, vol. 1, no. 1970, pp. 445–452, 1999.

[COO 05] COOPER G.M., STONE E.A., ASIMENOS G. *et al.*, "Distribution and intensity of constraint in mammalian genomic sequence", *Genome Research*, vol. 15, no. 7, pp. 901–913, 2005.

[CRI 58] CRICK F.H., "On protein synthesis", *Symposia of the Society for Experimental Biology*, vol. 12, pp. 138–163, 1958.

[CRO 04] CROOKS G.E., HON G., CHANDONIA J.M. *et al.*, "WebLogo: a sequence logo generator", *Genome Research*, vol. 14, no. 6, pp. 1188–1190, 2004.

[DAG 15] D'AGOSTINO D., PASQUALE G., MERELLI I., "A fine-grained CUDA implementation of the multi-objective evolutionary approach NSGA-II: potential impact for computational and systems biology applications", *Lecture Notes in Computer Science (including subseries Lecture Notes in Artificial Intelligence and Lecture Notes in Bioinformatics)*, pp. 273–284, 2015.

[DAL 12] DALQUEN D.A., ANISIMOVA M., GONNET G.H. *et al.*, "ALF-A simulation framework for genome evolution", *Molecular Biology and Evolution*, vol. 29, no. 4, pp. 1115–1123, 2012.

[DAR 04a] DARLING A.E., MAU B., BLATTNER F.R. *et al.*, "GRIL: genome rearrangement and inversion locator", *Bioinformatics*, vol. 20, no. 1, pp. 122–124, 2004.

[DAR 04b] DARLING A.E., MAU B., BLATTNER F.R. *et al.*, "Mauve: multiple alignment of conserved genomic sequence with rearrangements", *Genome Research*, vol. 14, no. 7, pp. 1394–1403, 2004.

[DAR 10] DARLING A.E., MAU B., PERNA N.T., "Progressivemauve: multiple genome alignment with gene gain, loss and rearrangement", *PLoS ONE*, vol. 5, no. 6, pp. e11147 2010.

[DAY 78] DAYHOFF M., SCHWARTZ R.M., ORCUTT B.C., "A model of evolutionary change in proteins", in *Atlas of Protein Sequence and Structure*, National Biomedical Research Foundation, Silver Spring, Maryland, USA, pp. 345–352, 1978.

[DEL 99] DELCHER A.L., KASIF S, FLEISCHMANN R.D. *et al.*, "Alignment of whole genomes", *Nucleic Acids Research*, vol. 27, no. 11, pp. 2369–2376, 1999.

[DEN 11] DENG X., CHENG J., "MSACompro: protein multiple sequence alignment using predicted secondary structure, solvent accessibility, and residue-residue contacts", *BMC Bioinformatics*, vol. 12, no. 1, p. 472, 2011.

[DEN 14] DENTON J.F, LUGO-MARTINEZ J., TUCKER A.E. *et al.*, "Extensive error in the number of genes inferred from draft genome assemblies", *PLoS Computational Biology*, vol. 10, no. 12, pp. e1003998, 2014.

[DEP 05] DE PARSEVAL N., HEIDMANN T., "Human endogenous retroviruses: from infectious elements to human genes", *Cytogenetic and Genome Research*, vol. 110, nos. 1–4, pp. 318–32, 2005.

[DES 10] DESSIMOZ C., GIL M., "Phylogenetic assessment of alignments reveals neglected tree signal in gaps", *Genome Biology*, vol. 11, no. 4, p. R37, 2010.

[DEW 07] DEWEY C.N., "Aligning multiple whole genomes with Mercator and MAVID", *Methods in Molecular Biology*, vol. 395, pp. 221–236, 2007.

[DEW 12] DEWEY C.N., "Whole-genome alignment", *Methods in Molecular Biology*, vol. 855, pp. 237–257, 2012.

[DEW 06] DEWEY C.N., PACHTER L., "Evolution at the nucleotide level: the problem of multiple whole-genome alignment", *Human Molecular Genetics*, Spec No 1, pp. R51–R56, 2006.

[DIT 10] DI TOMMASO P., OROBITG M., GUIRADO F. *et al.*, "Cloud-Coffee: Implementation of a parallel consistency-based multiple alignment algorithm in the T-coffee package and its benchmarking on the Amazon Elastic-Cloud", *Bioinformatics*, vol. 26, no. 15, pp. 1903–1904, 2010.

[DO 05] DO C.B., MAHABHASHYAM M., BRUDNO M.S. *et al.*, "ProbCons: probabilistic consistency-based multiple sequence alignment", *Genome Research*, vol. 15, no. 2, pp. 330–340, 2005.

[DON 09] DONTHU R., LEWIN H.A., LARKIN D.M., "SyntenyTracker: a tool for defining homologous synteny blocks using radiation hybrid maps and whole-genome sequence", *BMC Research Notes*, vol. 2, p. 148, 2009.

[DOO 86] DOOLITTLE R.F., *Of URFs and ORFs: A Primer on How to Analyze Derived Amino Acid Sequences*, University Science Books, Mill Valley, 1986.

[DRI 14] DRILLON G., CARBONE A., FISCHER G., "SynChro: a fast and easy tool to reconstruct and visualize synteny blocks along eukaryotic chromosomes", *PLoS ONE*, vol. 9, no. 3, p. e92621, 2014.

[DRO 15] DROZDETSKIY A., COLE C., PROCTER J. *et al.*, "JPred4: a protein secondary structure prediction server", *Nucleic Acids Research*, vol. 43, no. W1, pp. W389–W394, 2015.

[EAR 14] EARL D., NGUYEN N., HICKEY G. *et al.*, "Alignathon: a competitive assessment of whole-genome alignment methods", *Genome Research*, vol. 24, no. 12, pp. 2077–2089, 2014.

[EDD 98] EDDY S.R., "Profile hidden Markov models", *Bioinformatics*, vol. 14, no. 9, pp. 755–763, 1998.

[EDG 04] EDGAR R.C., "MUSCLE: multiple sequence alignment with high accuracy and high throughput", *Nucleic Acids Research*, vol. 32, no. 5, pp. 1792–1797, 2004.

[EL 13] EL-METWALLY S., HAMZA T., ZAKARIA M. *et al.*, "Next-generation sequence assembly: four stages of data processing and computational challenges", *PLoS Computational Biology*, vol. 9, no. 12, p. e1003345, 2013.

[ENC 07] ENCODE PROJECT CONSORTIUM, "Identification and analysis of functional elements in 1% of the human genome by the ENCODE pilot project", *Nature*, vol. 447, pp. 799–816, 2007.

[ESM 15] ESMAIELBEIKI R., KRAWCZYK K., KNAPP B. *et al.*, "Progress and challenges in predicting protein interfaces", *Briefings in Bioinformatics*, vol. 17, no. 1, pp. 117–131, 2015.

[FEL 04] FELSENSTEIN J., "Inferring phylogenies", *American Journal of Human Genetics*, vol. 74, no. 5, p. 1074, 2004.

[FEN 87] FENG D.F., DOOLITTLE R.F., "Progressive sequence alignment as a prerequisite to correct phylogenetic trees", *Journal of Molecular Evolution*, vol. 25, no. 4, pp. 351–360, 1987.

[FIN 15] FINN RD., COGGILL P., EBERHARDT R.Y. *et al.*, "The Pfam protein families database: towards a more sustainable future", *Nucleic Acids Research*, vol. 44, pp. D279–D285, 2015.

[FLE 05] FLEISSNER R., METZLER D., von HAESELER A., "Simultaneous statistical multiple alignment and phylogeny reconstruction", *Systematic Biology*, vol. 54, no. 4, pp. 548–561, 2005.

[FOR 15] FORTERRE P., "The universal tree of life: an update", *Frontiers in Microbiology*, vol. 6, p. 717, 2015.

[FOX 15] FOX G., SIEVERS F., HIGGINS D.G., "Using *de novo* protein structure predictions to measure the quality of very large multiple sequence alignments", *Bioinformatics*, vol. 32, no. 6, pp. 814–820, 2015.

[FRE 14] FREBOURG T., "The challenge for the next generation of medical geneticists", *Human Mutation*, vol. 35, no. 8, pp. 909–911, 2014.

[GAL 09] GALLIEN S., PERRODOU E., CARAPITO C. *et al.*, "Ortho-proteogenomics: multiple proteomes investigation through orthology and a new MS-based protocol", *Genome Research*, vol. 19, no. 1, pp. 128–135, 2009.

[GAR 01] GARDEZI S.A., NGUYEN C., MALLOY P.J. *et al.*, "A rationale for treatment of hereditary vitamin D-resistant rickets with analogs of 1α,25-dihydroxyvitamin D3", *Journal of Biological Chemistry*, vol. 276, no. 31, pp. 29148–29156, 2001.

[GAR 05] GARDNER P., WILM A., WASHIETL S., "A benchmark of multiple sequence alignment programs upon structural RNAs", *Nucleic Acids Research*, vol. 33, no. 8, pp. 2433–2439, 2005.

[GAS 97] GASCUEL O., "BIONJ: an improved version of the NJ algorithm based on a simple model of sequence data", *Molecular Biology and Evolution*, vol. 14, no. 7, pp. 685–95, 1997.

[GON 07] GONDRO C., KINGHORN B.P., "A simple genetic algorithm for multiple sequence alignment", *Genetics and Molecular Research*, vol. 6, no. 4, pp. 964–982, 2007.

[GOO 16] GOODWIN S., MCPHERSON J., MCCOMBIE W., "Coming of age: ten years of next-generation sequencing technologies", *Nature Review Genetics*, vol. 17, pp. 333–351, 2016.

[GOT 90] GOTOH O., "Consistency of optimal sequence alignments", *Bulletin of Mathematical Biology*, vol. 52, no. 4, pp. 509–525, 1990.

[GOT 96] GOTOH O., "Significant improvement in accuracy of multiple protein sequence alignments by iterative refinement as assessed by reference to structural alignments", *Journal of Molecular Biology*, vol. 264, no. 4, pp. 823–838, 1996.

[GUD 14] GUDYŚ A., DEOROWICZ S., "QuickProbs – a fast multiple sequence alignment algorithm designed for graphics processors", *PLoS One*, vol. 9, no. 2, p. e88901, 2014.

[GUI 06] GUIGÓ R., FLICEK P., ABRIL J.F. *et al.*, "EGASP: the human ENCODE Genome Annotation Assessment Project", *Genome Biology*, vol. 7, no. suppl 1, p. S2, 2006.

[GUS 97] GUSFIELD D., *Algorithms on Strings, Trees, and Sequences: Computer Science and Computational Biology*, Cambridge University Press, USA, 1997.

[HAL 10] HALLEGGER M., LLORIAN M., SMITH C.W.J., "Alternative splicing: global insights: minireview", *FEBS Journal*, vol. 277, no. 4, pp. 856–866, 2010.

[HAR 09] HARROW J., NAGY A., REYMOND A. *et al.*, "Identifying protein-coding genes in genomic sequences", *Genome Biology*, vol. 10, no. 1, p. 201, 2009.

[HEI 90] HEIN J., "Unified approach to alignment and phylogenies", *Methods in Enzymology*, vol. 183, pp. 626–645, 1990.

[HEI 03] HEIN J., JENSEN J.L., PEDERSEN C.N.S., "Recursions for statistical multiple alignment", *Proceedings of the National Academy of Sciences USA*, vol. 100, no. 25, pp. 14960–14965, 2003.

[HEN 92] HENIKOFF S., HENIKOFF J., "Amino acid substitution matrices from protein blocks", *Proceedings of the National Academy of Sciences*, vol. 89, pp. 10915–10919, 1992.

[HER 99] HERTZ G.D., STORMO G.Z., "Identifying DNA and protein patterns with statistically significant alignments of multiple sequences", *Bioinformatics*, vol. 15, nos. 7–8, pp. 563–577, 1999.

[HER 14] HERMAN J.L., CHALLIS C.J., NOVÁK A. *et al.*, "Simultaneous Bayesian estimation of alignment and phylogeny under a joint model of protein sequence and structure", *Molecular Biology and Evolution*, vol. 31, no. 9, pp. 2251–2266, 2014.

[HOL 05] HOLBROOK S.R., "RNA structure: the long and the short of it", *Current Opinion in Structural Biology*, vol. 15, pp. 302–308, 2005.

[HOL 15] HOLLIDAY G.L., BAIROCH A., BAGOS P.G. *et al.*, "Key challenges for the creation and maintenance of specialist protein resources", *Proteins: Structure, Function and Bioinformatics*, vol. 83, no. 6, pp. 1005–1013, 2015.

[HUA 07] HUANG W., NEVINS J.R., OHLER U., "Phylogenetic simulation of promoter evolution: estimation and modeling of binding site turnover events and assessment of their impact on alignment tools", *Genome Biology*, vol. 8, no. 10, p. R225, 2007.

[HUB 11] HUBISZ M.J., POLLARD K.S., SIEPEL A., "Phastand Rphast: phylogenetic analysis with space/time models", *Briefings in Bioinformatics*, vol. 12, no. 1, pp. 41–51, 2011.

[HUN 12] HUNTER A.A., MACGREGOR A.B., SZABO T.O. *et al.*, "Yabi: an online research environment for grid, high performance and cloud computing", *Source Code for Biology and Medicine*, vol. 7, no. 1, p. 1, 2012.

[IAN 14] IANTORNO S., GORI K., GOLDMAN N. *et al.*, "Who watches the watchmen? An appraisal of benchmarks for multiple sequence alignment", *Methods in Molecular Biology*, vol. 1079, pp. 59–73, 2014.

[ISH 93] ISHIKAWA M., TOYA T., HOSHIDA M. *et al.*, "Multiple sequence alignment by parallel simulated annealing", *Computer Applications in the Biosciences*, vol. 9, no. 3, pp. 267–273, 1993.

[JEH 15] JEHL P., SIEVERS F., HIGGINS D.G., "OD-seq: outlier detection in multiple sequence alignments", *BMC Bioinformatics*, vol. 16, no. 1, p. 269, 2015.

[JOO 08] JOO K., LEE J., KIM I. *et al.*, "Multiple sequence alignment by conformational space annealing", *Biophysical Journal*, vol. 95, no. 10, pp. 4813–4819, 2008.

[JOR 15] JORDAN D.M., FRANGAKIS S.G., GOLZIO C. *et al.*, "Identification of cis-suppression of human disease mutations by comparative genomics", *Nature*, vol. 524, no. 7564, pp. 225–230, 2015.

[JOS 10] JOSSINET F., LUDWIG T., WESTHOF E., "Assemble: an interactive graphical tool to analyze and build RNA architectures at the 2D and 3D levels", *Bioinformatics*, vol. 26, no. 16, pp. 2057–2059, 2010.

[KAY 14] KAYA M., SARHAN A., ALHAJJ R., "Multiple sequence alignment with affine gap by using multi-objective genetic algorithm", *Computer Methods and Programs in Biomedicine*, vol. 114, no. 1, pp. 38–49, 2014.

[KAM 12] KAMAL A., MAHROOS M., SAYED A. *et al.*, "Parallel particle swarm optimization for global multiple sequence alignment", *Information Technology Journal*, vol. 11, no. 8, pp. 998–1006, 2012.

[KAR 90] KARLIN S., ALTSCHUL S.F., "Methods for assessing the statistical significance of molecular sequence features by using general scoring schemes", *Proceedings of the National Academy of Sciences USA*, vol. 87, no. 6, pp. 2264–2268, 1990.

[KAR 01] KARPLUS K., HU B., "Evaluation of protein multiple alignments by SAM-T99 using the BAliBASE multiple alignment test set", *Bioinformatics*, vol. 17, no. 8, pp. 713–20, 2001.

[KAT 02] KATOH K., MISAWA K., KUMA K. *et al.*, "MAFFT: a novel method for rapid multiple sequence alignment based on fast Fourier transform", *Nucleic Acids Research*, vol. 30, no. 14, pp. 3059–3066, 2002.

[KAT 07] KATOH K., TOH H., "PartTree: an algorithm to build an approximate tree from a large number of unaligned sequences", *Bioinformatics*, vol. 23, no. 3, pp. 372–374, 2007.

[KAT 08] KATOH K., TOH H., "Improved accuracy of multiple ncRNA alignment by incorporating structural information into a MAFFT-based framework", *BMC Bioinformatics*, vol. 9, p. 212, 2008.

[KAT 10] KATOH K., TOH H., "Parallelization of the MAFFT multiple sequence alignment program", *Bioinformatics*, vol. 26, no. 15, pp. 1899–1900, 2010.

[KAT 12] KATOH K., FRITH M.C., "Adding unaligned sequences into an existing alignment using MAFFT and LAST", *Bioinformatics*, vol. 28, no. 23, pp. 3144–3146, 2012.

[KAT 14] KATSONIS P., KOIRE A., WILSON S.J. *et al.*, "Single nucleotide variations: biological impact and theoretical interpretation", *Protein Science*, vol. 23, no. 12, pp. 1650–1666, 2014.

[KER 15] KERSEY P.J., ALLEN J.E., ARMEAN I. *et al.*, "Ensembl genomes 2016: more genomes, more complexity", *Nucleic Acids Research*, vol. 44, pp. 574–580, 2015.

[KHE 14] KHENOUSSI W., VANHOUTREVE R., POCH O. *et al.*, "SIBIS: a Bayesian model for inconsistent protein sequence estimation", *Bioinformatics*, vol. 30, no. 17, pp. 2432–2439, 2014.

[KHO 15] KHOR B.Y. *et al.*, "General overview on structure prediction of twilight-zone proteins", *Theoretical Biology and Medical Modelling*, vol. 12, no. 15, 2015.

[KIM 94] KIM J., PRAMANIK S., CHUNG M.J., "Multiple sequence alignment using simulated annealing", *Computer Applications in the Biosciences*, vol. 10, no. 4, pp. 419–426, 1994.

[KIM 10a] KIM J., SINHA S., "Towards realistic benchmarks for multiple alignments of non-coding sequences", *BMC Bioinformatics*, vol. 11, no. 1, p. 54, 2010.

[KIM 10b] KIM T., JOO H., "ClustalXeed: a GUI-based grid computation version for high performance and terabyte size multiple sequence alignment", *BMC Bioinformatics*, vol. 11, p. 467, 2010.

[KIM 11] KIM J., MA J., "PSAR: measuring multiple sequence alignment reliability by probabilistic sampling", *Nucleic Acids Research*, vol. 39, no. 15, pp. 6359–6368, 2011.

[KIM 14a] KIM N., LAING C., ELMETWALY S. *et al.*, "Graph-based sampling for approximating global helical topologies of RNA", *Proceedings of the National Academy of Sciences USA*, vol. 111 no. 11, pp. 4079–4084, 2014.

[KIM 14b] KIM J., MA J., "PSAR-align: improving multiple sequence alignment using probabilistic sampling", *Bioinformatics*, vol. 30, no. 7, pp. 1010–1012, 2014.

[KIM 16] KIM C., GUO H., KONG W. *et al.*, "Application of genotyping by sequencing technology to a variety of crop breeding programs", *Plant Science*, vol. 242, pp. 14–22, 2016.

[KOE 02] KOEHL P., LEVITT M., "Sequence variations within protein families are linearly related to structural variations", *Journal of Molecular Biology*, vol. 323, no. 3, pp. 551–562, 2002.

[KOO 02] KOONIN E.V., WOLF Y.I., KAREV G.P., "The structure of the protein universe and genome evolution", *Nature*, vol. 420, no. 6912, pp. 218–223, 2002.

[KOU 06] KOURANOV A., XIE L., DE LA CRUZ J. *et al.*, "The RCSB PDB information portal for structural genomics", *Nucleic Acids Research*, vol. 34, pp. D302–D305, 2006.

[KRA 12] KRAMPIS K., BOOTH T., CHAPMAN B. *et al.*, "Cloud BioLinux: pre-configured and on-demand bioinformatics computing for the genomics community", *BMC Bioinformatics*, vol. 13, no. 1, p. 42, 2012.

[KRO 94] KROGH A., BROWN M., MIAN I.S. *et al.*, "Hidden Markov models in computational biology: Applications to protein modeling". *Journal of Molecular Biology*, vol. 235, no. 5, pp. 1501–1531, 1994.

[LAN 07] LANDAN G., GRAUR D., "Heads or tails: a simple reliability check for multiple sequence alignments", *Molecular Biology and Evolution*, vol. 24, no. 6, pp. 1380–1383, 2007.

[LAS 05a] LASSMAN T., SONNHAMMER E., "Kalign – an accurate and fast multiple sequence alignment algorithm", *BMC Bioinformatics*, vol. 6, p. 298, 2005.

[LAS 05b] LASSMANN T., SONNHAMMER E.L., "Automatic assessment of alignment quality", *Nucleic Acids Research*, vol. 33, no. 22, pp. 7120–7128, 2005.

[LAS 09] LASSMANN T., FRINGS O., SONNHAMMER E.L.L., "Kalign2: high-performance multiple alignment of protein and nucleotide sequences allowing external features", *Nucleic Acids Research*, vol. 37, no. 3, pp. 858–865, 2009.

[LEC 01] LECOMPTE O., THOMPSON J.D., PLEWNIAK F. *et al.*, "Multiple alignment of complete sequences (MACS) in the post-genomic era", *Gene*, vol. 270, nos. 1–2, pp. 17–30, 2001.

[LEC 02] LECOMPTE O., RIPP R., THIERRY J.C. *et al.*, "Comparative analysis of ribosomal proteins in complete genomes: an example of reductive evolution at the domain scale", *Nucleic Acids Research*, vol. 30, no. 24, pp. 5382–5390, 2002.

[LEE 02] LEE C., GRASSO C., SHARLOW M.F., "Multiple sequence alignment using partial order graphs", *Bioinformatics*, vol. 18, no. 3, pp. 452–464, 2002.

[LEE 08] LEE ZJ., SU S.F., CHUANG C.C. *et al.*, "Genetic algorithm with ant colony optimization (GA-ACO) for multiple sequence alignment", *Applied Soft Computing*, vol. 8, no. 1, pp. 55–78, 2008.

[LEO 03] LEONTIS N.B., WESTHOF E., "Analysis of RNA motifs", *Current Opinion in Structural Biology*, vol. 13, no. 3, pp. 300–308, 2003.

[LI 03] LI K.B., "ClustalW-MPI: ClustalW analysis using distributed and parallel computing", *Bioinformatics*, vol. 19, no. 12, pp. 1585–1586, 2003.

[LIP 89] LIPMAN D.J., ALTSCHUL S.F., KECECIOGLU J.D., "A tool for multiple sequence alignment", *Proceedings of the National Academy of Sciences USA*, vol. 86, no. 12, pp. 4412–4415, 1989.

[LIU 09a] LIU K., RAGHAVAN S., NELESEN S. *et al.*, Rapid and accurate large-scale coestimation of sequence alignments and phylogenetic trees. *Science*, vol. 324, no. 5934, pp. 1561–1564, 2009.

[LIU 09b] LIU Y., SCHMIDT B., MASKELL D.L., "MSA-CUDA: multiple sequence alignment on graphics processing units with CUDA", *2009 20th IEEE International Conference on Application Specific Systems Architectures and Processors*, Boston, pp. 121–128, 2009.

[LIU 10] LIU Y., SCHMIDT B., MASKELL D.L., "MSAProbs: multiple sequence alignment based on pair hidden Markov models and partition function posterior probabilities", *Bioinformatics*, vol. 26, no. 16, pp. 1958–1964, 2010.

[LIU 12] LIU K., WARNOW T.J., HOLDER M.T. *et al.*, "SATe-II: very fast and accurate simultaneous estimation of multiple sequence alignments and phylogenetic trees", *Systematic Biology*, vol. 61, no. 1, pp. 90–106, 2012.

[LIV 93] LIVINGSTONE C., BARTON G., "Protein sequence alignments: a strategy for the hierarchical analysis of residue conservation", *Computer Applications in Biosciences*, vol. 9, no. 6, pp. 745–756, 1993.

[LOE 09] LOEWENSTEIN Y., RAIMONDO D., REDFERN O.C. *et al.*, "Protein function annotation by homology-based inference", *Genome Biology*, vol. 10, no. 2, p. 207, 2009.

[LÖY 05] LÖYTYNOJA A., GOLDMAN N., "An algorithm for progressive multiple alignment of sequences with insertions", *Proceedings of the National Academy of Sciences USA*, vol. 102, no. 30, pp. 10557–10562, 2005.

[LÖY 12] LÖYTYNOJA A., VILELLA A.J., GOLDMAN N., "Accurate extension of multiple sequence alignments using a phylogeny-aware graph algorithm", *Bioinformatics*, vol. 28, no. 13, pp. 1684–1691, 2012.

[LUA 15] LUA R.C., WILSON S.J., KONECKI D.M. *et al.*, "UET: a database of evolutionarily-predicted functional determinants of protein sequences that cluster as functional sites in protein structures", *Nucleic Acids Research*, vol. 44, no. D1, pp. D308–D312, 2015.

[LUN 03] LUNTER G., MIKLÓS I., SONG Y.S. *et al.*, 'An efficient algorithm for statistical multiple alignment on arbitrary phylogenetic trees", *Journal of Computational Biology*, vol. 10, no. 6, pp. 869–889, 2003.

[LUN 05] LUNTER G., MIKLÓS I., DRUMMOND A. *et al.*, "Bayesian coestimation of phylogeny and sequence alignment", *BMC Bioinformatics*, vol. 6, p. 83, 2005.

[LUN 08] LUNTER G., ROCCO A., MIMOUNI N. *et al.*, "Uncertainty in homology inferences: assessing and improving genomic sequence alignment", *Genome Research*, vol. 18, no. 2, pp. 298–309, 2008.

[LUT 91] LUTHY R., MCLACHLAN A.D., EISENBERG D., "Secondary structure-based profiles: use of structure-conserving scoring tables in searching protein sequence databases for structural similarities", *Proteins*, vol. 10, no. 3, pp. 229–239, 1991.

[LUU 12] LUU T.D., RUSU A., WALTER V. *et al.*, "KD4v: comprehensible knowledge discovery system for missense variant", *Nucleic Acids Research*, vol. 40, no. W1, pp. W71–W75, 2012.

[MA 02] MA B., TROMP J., LI M., "PatternHunter: faster and more sensitive homology search", *Bioinformatics*, vol. 18, no. 3, pp. 440–445, 2002.

[MAI 12] MAITRE O., KRÜGER F., QUERRY S. *et al.*, "EASEA: specification and execution of evolutionary algorithms on GPGPU", *Soft Computing*, vol. 16, no. 2, pp. 261–279, 2012.

[MAN 13] MANNING T., SLEATOR R.D., WALSH P., "Naturally selecting solutions: the use of genetic algorithms in bioinformatics", *Bioengineered*, vol. 4, no. 5, pp. 266–78, 2013.

[MAR 02] MARCHLER-BAUER A., PANCHENKO A.R., SHOEMAKER B.A. *et al.*, "CDD: a database of conserved domain alignments with links to domain three-dimensional structure", *Nucleic Acids Research*, vol. 30, no. 1, pp. 281–283, 2002.

[MCC 94] MCCLURE M., VASI T.K., FITCH W.M., "Comparative analysis of multiple protein-sequence alignment methods", *Molecular Biology and Evolution*, vol. 11, no. 4, pp. 571–592, 1994.

[MIK 02] MIKLÓS I., "An improved algorithm for statistical alignment of sequences related by a star tree", *Bulletin of Mathematical Biology*, vol. 64, no. 4, pp. 771–779, 2002.

[MIL 15] MILLS C.L., BEUNING P.J., ONDRECHEN M.J., "Biochemical functional predictions for protein structures of unknown or uncertain function", *Computational and Structural Biotechnology Journal*, vol. 13, pp. 182–191, 2015.

[MIR 15] MIRARAB S., NGUYEN N., GUO S. *et al.*, "PASTA: ultra-large multiple sequence alignment for nucleotide and amino-acid sequences", *Journal of Computational Biology*, vol. 22, no. 5, pp. 377–386, 2015.

[MIT 15] MITCHELL A., CHANG H.Y., DAUGHERTY L. *et al.*, "The InterPro protein families database: the classification resource after 15 years", *Nucleic Acids Research*, vol. 43, no. D1, pp. D213–D221, 2015.

[MOR 96] MORGENSTERN B., DRESS A., WERNER T., "Multiple DNA and protein sequence alignment based on segment-to-segment comparison", *Proceedings of the National Academy of Sciences USA*, vol. 93, no. 22, pp. 12098–12103, 1996.

[MOR 98] MORGENSTERN B., FRECH K., DRESS A. *et al.*, "DIALIGN: finding local similarities by multiple sequence alignment", *Bioinformatics*, vol. 14, no. 3, pp. 290–294, 1998.

[MOR 06] MORRISON D.A., "Multiple sequence alignment for phylogenetic purposes", *Australian Systematic Botany*, vol. 19, no. 6, pp. 479–539, 2006.

[MOR 12] MOREAU Y., TRANCHEVENT L.C., "Computational tools for prioritizing candidate genes: boosting disease gene discovery", *Nature Reviews Genetics*, vol. 13, no. 8, pp. 523–536, 2012.

[MOU 05a] MOULT J., "A decade of CASP: progress, bottlenecks and prognosis in protein structure prediction", *Current Opinion in Structural Biology*, vol. 15, no. 3, pp. 285–289, 2005.

[MOU 05b] MOURIER T., "Reverse transcription in genome evolution", *Cytogenetic and Genome Research*, vol. 110, nos. 1–4, pp. 56–62, 2005.

[MYE 88] MYERS E.W., MILLER W., "Optimal alignments in linear space", *Computer Applications in the Biosciences*, vol. 4, no. 1, pp. 11–17, 1988.

[NAZ 11] NAZNIN F., SARKER R., ESSAM D., "Vertical decomposition with genetic algorithm for multiple sequence alignment", *BMC Bioinformatics*, vol. 12, p. 353, 2011.

[NEE 70] NEEDLEMAN S.B., WUNSCH C.D., "A general method applicable to the search for similarities in the amino acid sequence of two proteins" *Journal of Molecular Biology*, vol. 48, no. 3, pp. 443–453, 1970.

[NG 00] NG P., HENIKOFF J.G., HENIKOFF S., "PHAT: a transmembrane-specific substitution matrix. Predicted hydrophobic and transmembrane", *Bioinformatics*, vol. 16, no. 9, pp. 760–766, 2000.

[NGU 03] NGUYEN H.D., YAMAMORI K., YOSHIHARA I. *et al.*, "Improved GA-based method for multiple protein sequence alignment", *Congress on Evolutionary Computation (CEC '03)*, pp. 1826–1832, 2003.

[NGU 15] NGUYEN N.D., MIRARAB S., KUMAR K. *et al.*, "Ultra-large alignments using phylogeny-aware profiles", *Genome Biology*, vol. 16, no. 1, p. 124, 2015.

[NOB 16] NOBILE M.S., CAZZANIGA P., TANGHERLONI A. *et al.*, "Graphics processing units in bioinformatics, computational biology and systems biology", *Briefings in Bioinformatics*, pp. 1–16, 2016.

[NOT 96] NOTREDAME C., HIGGINS D.G., "SAGA: sequence alignment by genetic algorithm", *Nucleic Acids Research*, vol. 24, no. 8, pp. 1515–1524, 1996.

[NOT 97] NOTREDAME C., O'BRIEN E.A., HIGGINS D.G., "RAGA: RNA sequence alignment by genetic algorithm", *Nucleic Acids Research*, vol. 25, no. 22, pp. 4570–80, 1997.

[NOT 98] NOTREDAME C., HOLM L., HIGGINS D.G., "COFFEE: an objective function for multiple sequence alignments", *Bioinformatics*, vol. 14, no. 5, pp. 407–422, 1998.

[NOT 00] NOTREDAME C., HIGGINS D.G., HERINGA J., "T-Coffee: a novel method for fast and accurate multiple sequence alignment", *Journal of Molecular Biology*, vol. 302, no. 1, pp. 205–217, 2000.

[NOV 08] NOVAK A., MIKLOS I., LYNGSO R. *et al.*, "StatAlign: an extendable software package for joint Bayesian estimation of alignments and evolutionary trees", *Bioinformatics*, vol. 24, no. 20, pp. 2403–2404, 2008.

[OCH 15] OCHOA D. JUAN D., VALENCIA A. *et al.*, "Detection of significant protein coevolution", *Bioinformatics*, vol. 31, no. 13, pp. 2166–2173, 2015.

[ORT 13] ORTUÑO F.M., VALENZUELA O., ROJAS F. *et al.*, "Optimizing multiple sequence alignments using a genetic algorithm based on three objectives: structural information, non-gaps percentage and totally conserved columns", *Bioinformatics*, vol. 29, no. 17, pp. 2112–21, 2013.

[PAR 08] PARISIEN M., MAJOR F., "The MC-Fold and MC-Sym pipeline infers RNA structure from sequence data", *Nature*, vol. 452, no. 7183, pp. 51–55, 2008.

[PAT 08] PATEN B., HERRERO J., BEAL K. *et al.*, "Enredo and Pecan: genome-wide mammalian consistency-based multiple alignment with paralogs", *Genome Research*, vol. 18, no. 11, pp. 1814–1828, 2008.

[PAT 11] PATEN B., EARL D., NGUYEN N. *et al.*, "Cactus: algorithms for genome multiple sequence alignment", *Genome Research*, vol. 21, no. 9, pp. 1512–1528, 2011.

[PEA 90] PEARSON W.R., "Rapid and sensitive sequence comparison with FASTP and FASTA", *Methods in Enzymology*, vol. 183, pp. 63–98, 1990.

[PEA 98] PEARSON W.R., "Empirical statistical estimates for sequence similarity searches", *Journal of Molecular Biology*, vol. 276, no. 1, pp. 71–84, 1998.

[PEI 01] PEI J., GRISHIN N.V., "AL2CO: calculation of positional conservation in a protein sequence alignment", *Bioinformatics*, vol. 17, no. 8, pp. 700–712, 2001.

[PEI 07] PEI J., GRISHIN N.V., "PROMALS: towards accurate multiple sequence alignments of distantly related proteins", *Bioinformatics*, vol. 23, no. 7, pp. 802–808, 2007.

[PEN 10] PENN O., PRIVMAN E., ASHKENAZY H. *et al.*, "GUIDANCE: a web server for assessing alignment confidence scores", *Nucleic Acids Research*, vol. 33, pp. W23–W28, 38, 2010.

[PEV 03] PEVZNER P., TESLER G., "Genome rearrangements in mammalian evolution: lessons from human and mouse genomes", *Genome Research*, vol. 13, no. 1, pp. 37–45, 2003.

[PHA 10] PHAM S.K., PEVZNER P.A., "DRIMM-Synteny: decomposing genomes into evolutionary conserved segments", *Bioinformatics*, vol. 26, no. 20, pp. 2509–2516, 2010.

[PLE 00] PLEWNIAK F., THOMPSON J.D., POCH O., "Ballast: blast post-processing based on locally conserved segments", *Bioinformatics*, vol. 16, no. 9, pp. 750–759, 2000.

[PÖH 05] PÖHLER D., WERNER N., STEINKAMP R. *et al.*, "Multiple alignment of genomic sequences using CHAOS, DIALIGN and ABC", *Nucleic Acids Research*, vol. 33, pp. W532–W534, 2005.

[POL 04] POLLARD D.A., BERGMAN C.M., STOYE J. *et al.*, "Benchmarking tools for the alignment of functional noncoding DNA", *BMC Bioinformatics*, vol. 5, p. 6, 2004.

[POL 14] POLIAKOV A., FOONG J., BRUDNO M. *et al.*, "GenomeVISTA – an integrated software package for whole-genome alignment and visualization", *Bioinformatics*, vol. 30, no. 18, pp. 2654–2655, 2014.

[POP 12] POPENDA M., SZACHNIUK M., ANTCZAK M. *et al.*, "Automated 3D structure composition for large RNAs", *Nucleic Acids Research*, vol. 40, no. 14, p. e112, 2012.

[PRA 06] PRABHAKAR S., POULIN F., SHOUKRY M. *et al.*, "Close sequence comparisons are sufficient to identify human cis-regulatory elements", *Genome Research*, vol. 16, no. 7, pp. 855–863, 2006.

[PRI 12] PRINS P., BELHACHEMI D., MÖLLER S. *et al.*, "Scalable computing for evolutionary genomics", *Methods in Molecular Biology*, vol. 856, pp. 529–545, 2012.

[PRO 12] PROSDOCIMI F., LINARD B., PONTAROTTI P. *et al.*, "Controversies in modern evolutionary biology: the imperative for error detection and quality control", *BMC Genomics*, vol. 13, p. 5, 2012.

[RAB 16] RABBANI B., NAKAOKA H., AKHONDZADEH S. *et al.*, "Next generation sequencing: implications in personalized medicine and pharmacogenomics", *Molecular Biosystem*, vol. 12, pp. 1818–1830, 2016.

[RAG 03] RAGHAVA G.P., SEARLE S.M., AUDLEY P.C. *et al.*, "OXBench: a benchmark for evaluation of protein multiple sequence alignment accuracy", *BMC Bioinformatics*, vol. 4, p. 47, 2003.

[RAP 04] RAPHAEL B., ZHI D., TANG H. *et al.*, "A novel method for multiple alignment of sequences with repeated and shuffled elements", *Genome Research*, vol. 14, no. 11, pp. 2336–2346, 2004.

[RAT 13] RATH EM., TESSIER D., CAMPBELL A.A. *et al.*, "A benchmark server using high resolution protein structure data, and benchmark results for membrane helix predictions", *BMC Bioinformatics*, vol. 14, no. 1, p. 111, 2013.

[ROC 00] ROCHEL N., WURTZ J.M., MITSCHLER A. *et al.*, "The crystal structure of the nuclear receptor for vitamin D bound to its natural ligand", *Molecular Cell*, vol. 5, no. 1, pp. 173–179, 2000.

[ROD 04] RODI D., MANDAVA S., MAKOWSKI L., "DIVAA: analysis of amino acid diversity in multiple aligned protein sequences", *Bioinformatics*, vol. 20, no. 18, pp. 3481–3489, 2004.

[ROS 06] ROSHAN U., LIVESAY D.R., "Probalign: multiple sequence alignment using partition function posterior probabilities", *Bioinformatics*, vol. 22, no. 22, pp. 2715–2721, 2006.

[ROS 11] ROSKIN K.M., PATEN B., HAUSSLER D., "Meta-alignment with crumble and prune: partitioning very large alignment problems for performance and parallelization", *BMC Bioinformatics*, vol. 12, p. 144, 2011.

[RUB 00] RUBIN G.M., YANDELL M.D., WORTMAN J.R. *et al.*, "Comparative genomics of the eukaryotes", *Science*, vol. 287, no. 5461, pp. 2204–2215, 2000.

[SAM 06] SAMMETH M., HERINGA J., "Global multiple-sequence alignment with repeats", *Proteins*, vol. 64, no. 1, pp. 263–274, 2006.

[SAN 75] SANKOFF D., "Minimal mutation trees of sequences", *SIAM Journal of Applied Mathematics*, 28, pp. 35–42, 1975.

[SCH 90] SCHNEIDER T.D., STEPHENS R.M., "Sequence logos: a new way to display consensus sequences", *Nucleic Acids Research*, vol. 18, no. 20, pp. 6097–6100, 1990.

[SCH 15] SCHRAIBER J.G., AKEY J.M., "Methods and models for unravelling human evolutionary history", *Nature Reviews Genetics*, vol. 16, no. 12, pp. 727–740, 2015.

[SHA 05] SHAPIRO J.A., "A 21st century view of evolution: genome system architecture, repetitive DNA, and natural genetic engineering", *Gene*, vol. 345, no. 1, pp. 91–100, 2005.

[SHY 04] SHYU C., SHENEMAN L., FOSTER J.A., "Multiple sequence alignment with evolutionary computation", *Genetic Programming and Evolvable Machines*, vol. 5, no. 2, pp. 121–144, 2004.

[SIE 11] SIEVERS F., WILM A., DINEEN D. *et al.*, "Fast, scalable generation of high-quality protein multiple sequence alignments using Clustal Omega", *Molecular Systems Biology*, vol. 7, no. 1, p. 539, 2011.

[SIE 13] SIEVERS F., DINEEN D., WILM A. *et al.*, "Making automated multiple alignments of very large numbers of protein sequences", *Bioinformatics*, vol. 29, no. 8, pp. 989–995, 2013.

[SIG 13] SIGRIST C.J.A. *et al.*, "New and continuing developments at PROSITE", *Nucleic Acids Research*, vol. 41, no. D1, pp. D344–D347, 2013.

[SIM 05] SIMOSSIS V.A., HERINGA J., "PRALINE: a multiple sequence alignment toolbox that integrates homology-extended and secondary structure information", *Nucleic Acids Research*, vol. 33, pp W289–W294, 2005.

[SMA 05] SMAGALA J.A., DAWSON E.D., MEHLMANN M. *et al.*, "ConFind: a robust tool for conserved sequence identification", *Bioinformatics*, vol. 21, no. 24, pp. 4420–4422, 2005.

[SMI 81] SMITH T.F., WATERMAN M.S., "Identification of common molecular subsequences", *Journal of Molecular Biology*, vol. 147, no. 1, pp. 195–197, 1981.

[SNE 73] SNEATH P.H.A., SOKAL R.R., *Numerical Taxonomy – The Principles and Practice of Numerical Classification*, W.H. Freeman, San Francisco, 1973.

[SÖD 05] SÖDING J., "Protein homology detection by HMM-HMM comparison", *Bioinformatics*, vol. 21, no. 7, pp. 951–960, 2005.

[SPE 15] SPEIR M.L., ZWEIG A.S., ROSENBLOOM K.R. *et al.*, "The UCSC Genome Browser database: 2016 update", *Nucleic Acids Research*, vol. 44, pp. D717–D725, 2015.

[STO 97] STOYE J., MOULTON V., DRESS A.W., "DCA: an efficient implementation of the divide-and-conquer approach to simultaneous multiple sequence alignment", *Computer Applications in the Biosciences*, vol. 13, pp. 625–626, 1997.

[SUB 08] SUBRAMANIAN A.R., KAUFMANN M., MORGENSTERN B., "DIALIGN-TX: greedy and progressive approaches for segment-based multiple sequence alignment", *Algorithms for Molecular Biology*, vol. 3, p. 6, 2008.

[SUC 06] SUCHARD M.A., REDELINGS B.D., "BAli-Phy: simultaneous Bayesian inference of alignment and phylogeny", *Bioinformatics*, vol. 22, no. 16, pp. 2047–2048, 2006.

[SZA 15] SZAFRANSKI K., ABRAHAM K.J., MEKHAIL K., "Non-coding RNA in neural function, disease, and aging", *Frontiers in Genetics*, vol. 6, p. 87, 2015.

[TAH 09] TAHERI J., ZOMAYA A.Y., "RBT-GA: a novel metaheuristic for solving the multiple sequence alignment problem", *BMC Genomics*, vol. 10, p. S10, 2009.

[TAN 15] TANG H., BOMHOFF M.D., BRIONES E. *et al.*, "SynFind: compiling syntenic regions across any set of genomes on demand", *Genome Biology and Evolution*, vol. 7, no. 12, pp. 3286–3298, 2015.

[TAY 87] TAYLOR W.R., "Multiple sequence alignment by a pairwise algorithm", *Computer Applications in Biosciences*, vol. 3, no. 2, pp. 81–87, 1987.

[THO 91] THORNE J.L., KISHINO H., FELSENSTEIN J., "An evolutionary model for maximum likelihood alignment of DNA sequences", *Journal of Molecular Evolution*, vol. 33, no. 2, pp. 114–124, 1991.

[THO 94] THOMPSON J.D., HIGGINS D., GIBSON T., "CLUSTAL W: improving the sensitivity of progressive multiple sequence alignment through sequence weighting, position-specific gap penalties and weight matrix choice", *Nucleic Acids Research*, vol. 22, no. 22, pp. 4673–4680, 1994.

[THO 95] THOMPSON J.D., "Introducing variable gap penalties to sequence alignment in linear space", *Computer Applications in Biosciences*, vol. 11, pp. 181–186, 1995.

[THO 97] THOMPSON J.D., GIBSON T.J., PLEWNIAK F. *et al.*, "The CLUSTAL_X windows interface: flexible strategies for multiple sequence alignment aided by quality analysis tools", *Nucleic Acids Research*, vol. 25, no. 24, pp. 4876–4882, 1997.

[THO 99a] THOMPSON J.D., PLEWNIAK F., POCH O., "BAliBASE: a benchmark alignment database for the evaluation of multiple alignment programs", *Bioinformatics*, vol. 15, no. 1, pp. 87–88, 1999.

[THO 99b] THOMPSON J.D., PLEWNIAK F., POCH O., "A comprehensive comparison of multiple sequence alignment programs", *Nucleic Acids Research*, vol. 27, no. 13, pp. 2682–2690, 1999.

[THO 00] THOMPSON J.D., PLEWNIAK F., THIERRY J *et al.*, "DbClustal: rapid and reliable global multiple alignments of protein sequences detected by database searches", *Nucleic Acids Research*, vol. 28, no. 15, pp. 2919–2926, 2000.

[THO 01] THOMPSON J.D., PLEWNIAK F., RIPP R. *et al.*, "Towards a reliable objective function for multiple sequence alignments", *Journal of Molecular Biology*, vol. 314, no. 4, pp. 937–51, 2001.

[THO 03] THOMPSON J.D., THIERRY J.C., POCH O., "RASCAL: rapid scanning and correction of multiple sequence alignments", *Bioinformatics*, vol. 19, no. 9, pp. 1155–1161, 2003.

[THO 05] THOMPSON J.D., KOEHL P., RIPP R. *et al.*, "BAliBASE 3.0: latest developments of the multiple sequence alignment benchmark", *Proteins: Structure, Function and Genetics*, vol. 61, no. 1, pp. 127–136, 2005.

[THO 11] THOMPSON J.D., PLEWNIAK F., POCH O. *et al.*, "A comprehensive benchmark study of multiple sequence alignment methods: current challenges and future perspectives", *PLoS One*, vol. 6, no. 3, p. e18093, 2011.

[TUI 10] TUITE M.F., SERIO T.R., "The prion hypothesis: from biological anomaly to basic regulatory mechanism", *Nature Reviews Molecular Cell Biology*, vol. 11, no. 12, pp. 823–833, 2010.

[VAL 14] VALLENET D., ENGELEN S., MORNICO D. *et al.*, "MicroScope: a platform for microbial genome annotation and comparative genomics", *Database*, vol. 2009, 2014.

[VAN 05] VAN DOMSELAAR G.H., STOTHARD P., SHRIVASTAVA S. *et al.*, "BASys: a web server for automated bacterial genome annotation", *Nucleic Acids Research*, vol. 33, pp. W455–459, 2005.

[VAN 16] VANHOUTREVE R., KRESS A., LEGRAND B. *et al.*, "LEON-BIS: multiple alignment evaluation of sequence neighbours using a Bayesian inference system", *BMC Bioinformatics*, vol. 17, p. 271, 2016.

[VIN 97] VINGRON M., VON HAESELER A., "Towards integration of multiple alignment and phylogenetic tree construction", *Journal of Computational Biology*, vol. 4, no. 1, pp. 23–34, 1997.

[WAN 94] WANG L., JIANG T., "On the complexity of multiple sequence alignment", *Journal of Computational Biology*, vol. 1, no. 4, pp. 337–348, 1994.

[WAS 08] WASS M.N., STERNBERG M.J.E., "ConFunc – functional annotation in the twilight zone", *Bioinformatics*, vol. 24, no. 6, pp. 798–806, 2008.

[WAT 05] WATSON J.D., LASKOWSKI R.A., THORNTON J.M., "Predicting protein function from sequence and structural data", *Current Opinion in Structural Biology*, vol. 15, no. 3, pp. 275–284, 2005.

[WAT 09] WATERHOUSE A.M., PROCTER J.B., MARTIN D.M.A. *et al.*, "Jalview Version 2-A multiple sequence alignment editor and analysis workbench", *Bioinformatics*, vol. 25, no. 9, pp. 1189–1191, 2009.

[WES 12] WESTESSON O., BARQUIST L., HOLMES I., "HandAlign: Bayesian multiple sequence alignment, phylogeny and ancestral reconstruction", *Bioinformatics*, vol. 28, no. 8, pp. 1170–1171, 2012.

[WHE 07] WHEELER T.J., KECECIOGLU J.D., "Multiple alignment by aligning alignments", *Bioinformatics*, vol. 23, no. 13, pp. i559–568, 2007.

[WIL 08] WILM A., HIGGINS D.G., NOTREDAME C., "R-Coffee: a method for multiple alignment of non-coding RNA", *Nucleic Acids Research*, vol. 36, no. 9, pp. W10–13, 2008.

[WOE 93] WOESE C.R., PACE N.R., "Probing RNA structure, function and history by comparative analysis", *The RNA World*, Cold Spring Harbor Laboratory Press, 1993.

[WOE 00] WOESE C.R., "Interpreting the universal phylogenetic tree", *Proceedings of the National Academy of Sciences USA*, vol. 97, no. 15, pp. 8392–8396, 2000.

[WRA 04] WRABL J.O., GRISHIN N.V., "Gaps in structurally similar proteins: towards improvement of multiple sequence alignment", *Proteins: Structure, Function and Genetics*, vol. 54, no. 1, pp. 71–87, 2004.

[XU 14] XU X., ZHAO P., CHEN S.J., "Vfold: a web server for RNA structure and folding thermodynamics prediction", PLoS One, vol. 9, no. 9, p. e107504, 2014.

[XU 16] XU Y., CHOU K., "Recent progress in predicting posttranslational modification sites in proteins", Current Topics in Medicinal Chemistry, vol. 16, no. 6, pp. 591–603, 2016.

[YAM 16] YAMADA K., TOMII K., "Application of the MAFFT sequence alignment program to large data – reexamination of the usefulness of chained guide trees", Bioinformatics, forthcoming, 2016.

[YU 14] YU Y.K., CAPRA J.A., STOJMIROVIC A. et al., "Log-odds sequence logos", Bioinformatics, vol. 31, no. 3, pp. 324–331, 2014.

[ZHA 97] ZHANG C., WONG A.K., "A genetic algorithm for multiple molecular sequence alignment", Computer Applications in Bioscience, vol. 13, no. 6, pp. 565–81, 1997.

[ZHO 09] ZHOU Y., TAN Y., "GPU-based parallel particle swarm optimization", IEEE Congress on Evolutionary Computation, CEC, pp. 1493–1500, 2009.

[ZHU 15] ZHU X., LI K., SALAH A. et al., "Parallel implementation of MAFFT on CUDA-enabled graphics hardware", IEEE/ACM Transactions on Computational Biology and Bioinformatics, vol. 12, pp. 205–218, 2015.

[ZIC 15] ZICKMANN F., RENARD B.Y., "IPred – integrating ab initio and evidence based gene predictions to improve prediction accuracy", BMC Genomics, vol. 16, p. 134, 2015.

[ZOL 07] ZOLA J., YANG X., ROSPONDEK S. et al., "Parallel T-Coffee: a parallel multiple sequence aligner", ISCA PDCS '07, pp. 248–253, 2007.

Index